Pneuma and Logos

Pneuma and Logos

The Role of the Spirit in Biblical Hermeneutics

JOHN W. WYCKOFF

WIPF & STOCK · Eugene, Oregon

PNEUMA AND LOGOS
The Role of the Spirit in Biblical Hermeneutics

Wipf & Stock
An Imprint of Wipf and Stock Publishers
199 W. 8th Ave., Suite 3
Eugene, OR 97401
www.wipfandstock.com

ISBN 13: 978-1-60899-483-0

Manufactured in the U.S.A.

I dedicate this book to
my beloved wife, Myrna,
my faithful companion of forty years

Contents

Abbreviations

BDT	*Baker's Dictionary of Theology*
BSac	*Bibliotheca Sacra*
CBQ	*Catholic Biblical Quarterly*
CH	*Church History*
CTJ	*Calvin Theological Journal*
CWS	*Classics of Western Spirituality*
diss.	dissertation
EBC	Expositor's Bible Commentary
ed(s)	editor(s); edition
EDT	*Evangelical Dictionary of Theology*
et al.	*et alii* (and others)
EvQ	*Evangelical Quarterly*
ExAud	*Ex auditu*
GBS	Guides for Biblical Scholarship
i.e.	*id est* (that is)
Int	*Interpretation*
JR	*Journal of Religion*
NBD	*New Bible Dictionary*
NICNT	New International Commentary on the New Testament
NTS	*New Testament Studies*
RefR	*Reformed Review*
SDS	Studies in Dogmatics Series

SJT	*Scottish Journal of Theology*
SPEP	*Northwestern University Studies in Phenomenology and Existential Philosophy*
SVTQ	*St. Vladimir's Theological Quarterly*
TDNT	*Theological Dictionary of the New Testament*
trans.	translator, translated by
TS	*Theological Studies*
TynBul	*Tyndale Bulletin*
v./vv.	verse/verses
vol./vols.	volume/volumes
WDCT	*Westminster Dictionary of Christian Theology*

Foreword

by James D. Hernando

JOHN WYCKOFF'S 1990 PH.D. DISSERTATION has finally come to print and is long overdue. In fact, it is perplexing how a scholarly treatise on such an intriguing topic was not snatched up by a publishing house in search of book candidates on controversial topics of perennial interest. *Pneuma and Logos* is just such a book. It sharply focuses on a hermeneutical question that has commanded the attention of church fathers and theologians from the earliest times of theological reflection in the Church. Simply put the question is, "Does the Holy Spirit have a role to play in the interpretive process called *hermeneutics*?" A necessary follow-up question, if the first is answered in the affirmative, is "How and to what extent does the Holy Spirit facilitate a person's understanding of the Scriptures?"

Scholars and teachers interested in biblical hermeneutics are well aware that the central focus of this book is one well-worth considering, if for no other reason than the Bible itself raises the question in passages like 1 Cor 2:10–15 and 2 Cor 5:5–17, not to mention John's gospel where the "teaching" function of the Holy Spirit is amply attested. Oddly, seldom do hermeneutical textbooks contain a substantive treatment of the question at hand. In his introduction to the problem, Wyckoff describes a paradox. Scholars representing a wide spectrum of Christian tradition recognize the importance and challenges of biblical hermeneutics. Many of these hold to a high view of Scripture as the inspired Word of God and posit an active role of the Holy Spirit in its production. Yet pneumatology has received short *Schrift* when it comes to hermeneutical reflection. Our author seeks not only to speak to this neglect, but make a major move toward remedying it.

In the space of five compact and well-constructed chapters, Wyckoff conducts a historically-informed exercise in philosophical theology around the issue of the Holy Spirit's relationship to biblical hermeneutics. Chapter one clearly states and defines the nature of the problem, establishes the need for the present study, circumscribes its scope and describes its internal organization. Admittedly the complex and multifaceted character of hermeneutics will raise a host of issues and questions beyond the scope of this book, but the author is determined to stay focused on the primary question which he argues deserves our singular attention.

Chapter 2 surveys the history of biblical interpretation from Early Church to the Reformation; the Reformation to the Enlightenment; and the Enlightenment to mid-20th century. As a teacher I thoroughly enjoyed this helpful historical survey of the Church's consideration of the Holy Spirit's relationship to hermeneutics because it also serves as a primer to the field of *historical hermeneutics* in general. It provides a needed supplement to most textbooks in hermeneutics. Wyckoff conducts an overview of the major schools of biblical interpretation, their major figures and a succinct statement of their contribution to the field. Students will especially appreciate the summaries that appear after each historical period and the author's conclusions at the end of the chapter. He lingers over major figures such as Origen, Chrysostom, Augustine, Aquinas, Luther, Calvin, Turretin, Schleiermacher, Barth etc. to highlight their specific contributions to hermeneutics and specifically how they related the Spirit to a believer's understanding of Scripture. Numerous choice quotes from the early Church Fathers and theologians demonstrate their high view of Scripture owing to their conviction of its divine origin and inspiration. It is this *theological* conviction which naturally led to their *hermeneutical* consideration of how the Holy Spirit continues to function as a mediator of Divine truth through the Scriptures. Nevertheless, while most affirmed this role of the Holy Spirit, some denied or deemphasized it. The author provides trenchant insight into why this was so by revealing the theological, philosophical and epistemological presuppositions at work.

The historical background supplied by Chapter 2 is just the foundation and perspective needed to evaluate contemporary scholars in their treatment of this same question. Wyckoff samples widely from a broad stream of Christian tradition, including numerous Protestant and Catholic scholars. Nevertheless, he sharpens his focus on evangelical scholars who view the Scripture as the work of the Holy Spirit through inspiration. The question to examine is whether these same scholars posit a role for the Spirit in the hermeneutical process. He broadly divides these scholars into two camps: those that deny or limit the Holy Spirit's role and those that affirm and emphasize it. Once again, which camp one finds him/herself in depends on theological and philosophical presuppositions regarding the nature of Scripture itself and how one understands what transpires when a person reads or seeks to understand it. Our author exposes us to scholars who all, to one degree or another, affirm that the Holy Spirit has a place at the hermeneutical table. However, they fail to agree concerning his portion and exact placement. Wyckoff next explores why these scholars posit the necessity of the Spirit in the hermeneutical enterprise. The answer to the question is found in the sinfulness of man and its inherent limitations, limitations that are both ontological and epistemological, limitations that must be overcome if God is to communicate his divine truth. What follows is a carefully nuanced theological discussion of the epistemological role of the Spirit as it relates to and merges with the doctrines of divine inspiration and illumination by the Spirit. The consensus that emerges is one that clearly affirms the Spirit's contemporary role in aiding humanity in understanding the Scriptures. What becomes equally clear is that, due to the transcendent reality being considered, scholars find it nearly impossible to conceptualize or describe this role with any specificity. Dr. Wyckoff should be commended for venturing out and working toward conceptualization no matter how elusive or difficult.

Wyckoff devotes the lion's share of Chapter 3 to hermeneutical questions and controversial issues that erupt when asking, "If the Holy Spirit assists the reader in understanding Scripture, . . . how does the message differ from that understood by ordinary means?" (p. 65). The student of hermeneutics is introduced to such issues as the *sensus plenior* and its relationship to the message intended by the author, the challenges of hermeneutical methods that deny the need or relevance of original authorial intent, and mediating positions that seek to affirm the importance of both the author's meaning and the "God-intended meaning" supplied by the Spirit. Some may balk at the author's attempt to find a satisfactory position that allows for "special revelation" mediated by the Spirit, one which the author "may or may not have fully understood." Our anxiety should subside when we read Wyckoff's qualifier. Such special revelation via the Spirit enables the interpreter "to gain fresh insight into the meaning of the text" . . . but "this does not include new revelation" that is divorced from and alien to the meaning of the text originally intended by the biblical author. Nevertheless, our author works hard to articulate the character of this "special revelation." A variety of terminology is used: "ultracognitive". . . beyond ordinary human comprehension." It is what Torrance called "Supreme Truth" that constitutes Scripture's "spiritual meaning." It communicates an *experiential* knowledge of the heart (p. 72) which is inherently *spiritual* (*pneumatikos*), calling for the mediatory role of the Holy Spirit. Ultimately the illumination via the Spirit communicates the person and work of Christ himself. Consistent with Johannine pneumatology, the Spirit's illumination is fundamentally Christocentric.

Even if convinced that the Spirit has the hermeneutical role described above, the question of HOW still remains. Our author devotes most of the remaining two chapters in responding to the challenge of explaining how the Sprit provides illumination. While admitting he is seeking to explain a "mystery" and attempting to put into words the ineffable, he nonetheless asserts that incomplete and/or imperfect conceptualization and articulation is better than none at all. And so Wyckoff looks to the metaphors of Scripture itself as a window into the mystery of pneumatic activity in the hermeneutical task. He lists such verbal metaphors as "enlightening"(Eph 1:19), "guiding" (John 16:13) and "unveiling" (2 Cor 3:12) as instructive and discusses models that help conceptualize how the Spirit conveys or transmits understanding. After critiquing and rejecting two inferior models, the author adopts the "teacher" metaphor and model as the most helpful and instructive. His choice is prompted by the prevalence of this metaphor in Scripture and the epistemological contexts that surround it. It also underscores the cooperative participation between interpreter and the Holy Spirit in the hermeneutical process. The testimony of numerous scholars establishes a broad consensus that it is a collaborative effort that does not marginalize the input and involvement of the Holy Spirit or the interpreter. Moreover, the task is synergistic in the fact that Spirit and his illumination works "through the normal processes of human understanding" – read the critical procedures of biblical exegesis and hermeneutical principles. Among these principles the one that I believe is ripe for elaboration and further reflection is "responsiveness." This principle points to the Spirit's impact on the reader volitionally. What is not completely clear is whether the reader/interpreter's response is an internal or external one, and whether it is a prerequisite for illumination or its attendant result.

Who are candidates for the Spirit's illumination of Scripture? *Believers* of course are the primary recipients, Wyckoff acknowledges, but what about non-believers? His answer is one that requires careful theological analysis or readers might be led to false conclusions, perhaps by what is not stated more than what is. The author states plainly that some measure of the Spirit's enlightenment must be available to unbelievers or the gospel message would then have remained veiled and hidden from their understanding. How then could they be converted? Confusion may result when we fail to distinguish contexts. Unbelievers confronted with the gospel on the way to conversion, are not in the same situation as believers, regenerated by the Spirit, seeking to understand God's Word.

Wyckoff's most novel and original work is clearly found in Chapter 4 where he presents a model and method for conceptualizing the work of the Spirit in the process of interpretation. Here is where he combines models of teaching gleaned from educational theory with the "Teacher" metaphor for the work of the Spirit found in Scripture. Educators acknowledge three basic teaching/learning paradigms: *authoritative*, *laissez-faire*, and *facilitator*. Our author carefully describes the role of the teacher, the mode and manner of teaching, and the anticipated outcomes or results under each paradigm. He then explores how one would view the work of the Spirit as Teacher under each paradigm as it relates to the scripture-reader and the spiritual results of that educational transaction. The teaching/learning paradigm of *facilitator* is shown to be most reflective of the Spirit's work in the collaborative hermeneutical enterprise previously discussed. Educators and theologians alike will resonate with his conclusion that this paradigm facilitates learning that results in a higher order of knowledge, one that is both experiential and transformational.

John Wyckoff has done the Church a great service in fostering theological and hermeneutical reflection on a timeless topic of continuing relevance. Pentecostals and Charismatics, in particular, ought to be grateful for his strong insistence that hermeneutics is fundamentally *pneumatic*, the Spirit retaining an active role in the interpretive process, one that is in continuity with (albeit distinct from) his inspiration of the Scriptures. Moreover, our author is to be congratulated for his courage to deal with the tough and sticky hermeneutical and theological questions that arise when one seeks to conceptualize and articulate the transcendent reality and work of the Spirit. In Chapter 5 he summarizes the results of his study with a humble acknowledgement of its limits and anticipates some criticism that is sure to follow. Nevertheless, he has pushed us forward in theological and hermeneutical reflection and refined and clarified our task of defining the Spirit's role in biblical interpretation. He's given us a workable model (Spirit as Teacher) that helps, but does not exhaust the nature of the task. He has even dared broach the subject of "how" the Spirit's illumination works. The most daring aspect of his proposal is to distinguish interpretation through normal human intellect on the one hand, and that aided by the Spirit's illumination on the other. In the latter he hints at a different epistemology that produces not only a "contemporary significance" of Scripture, but a divine-human transaction whereby the reader-interpreter experiences the being of God himself. As controversial and abstract as this proposal may be, it is one cogently argued within the parameters of theological orthodoxy and anticipated or confirmed by more than a few theologians.

Wyckoff is his own best critic and he ends his work with suggestions to refine and amend his proposal. The reader is challenged not only to critique that proposal, but through additional research refine it or even offer one of his/her own. In *Pneuma and Logos* Dr. Wyckoff has presented us with an illuminating work, an engaging proposal and a provocative challenge.

Preface

CURRENTLY, I AM GRADUATE Chair of Theological Studies and Professor of Bible and Theology at Southwestern Assemblies of God University in Waxahachie, Texas. My tenure as Professor of Bible and Theology here began in the fall of 1976. At that time, the school was very small and its curriculum was very limited. Although biblical interpretation was modeled and guided in the Bible courses, the closest thing to a course specifically on how to study and interpret Scripture, was a course entitled "Bibliology and Hermeneutics." But, that course was focused especially on how the Bible was produced and included very little instruction on how to understand and interpret Scripture. Recognizing the need for training in proper interpretation of Scripture, the Dean assigned this course to me and instructed me to develop it into a beginning level hermeneutics course. This was the beginning of my personal journey in the study of this very important field. And, being a Pentecostal, it was inevitable that I would soon be interested in the role of the Holy Spirit in the hermeneutical process.

The development of hermeneutics as a discipline is directly and particularly related to the need to understand the biblical text and determine its relevance to the present day human situation. Since the earliest developments of biblical interpretation, hermeneuts have held that divine activity is associated with the human effort of understanding this divine revelation. Contemporary biblical scholars also usually see biblical hermeneutics as a cooperative endeavor involving both human scholarship and Spirit enlightenment. However, these scholars usually give only brief, passing acknowledgment to this idea. Thus, during my doctorial studies at Baylor University, for my dissertation project, I decided to devote my efforts to investigating the relationship of the Holy Spirit to biblical hermeneutics. This book is the product of that project.

The focus of this work is threefold. First, it shows that the idea of the Holy Spirit's role in biblical hermeneutics is faithful to the Christian tradition. Second, it considers to what extent this idea is logically consistent with contemporary theological thought. Third, it presents and discusses models for conceptualizing and articulating the Holy Spirit's relationship to the hermeneutical process. The Holy Spirit's activity and the results of his involvement are necessarily described metaphorically. The models associated with this metaphorical language provide vehicles for furthering discourse on the Spirit's relationship to hermeneutics.

I want to thank Dr. Bob Patterson, my dissertation committee chair, and the Baylor University religion faculty who instructed and guided me during my doctorial studies there. I also, want to thank the administration and faculty at Southwestern Assemblies of God University who supported me and allowed special time away from my teaching duties in order to compete the dissertation project. Finally, I want to thank my wife, Myrna; our son, Ryan; and, our daughter, Bethany for their understanding and encouragement, without which I could not have endured the long, grueling doctorial studies years.

John W. Wyckoff
Waxahachie, Texas
May 2010

1

Introduction

THE PROBLEM

Introduction to the Problem

T HE TASK OF UNDERSTANDING and interpreting Scripture ever presses itself upon those who work in the various areas related to biblical studies. The current increase in the number of books and articles on hermeneutics indicates the recent surge of interest in this discipline. These books and articles not only cover the general field of hermeneutics, but they also address various special topics and issues. One issue often mentioned but seldom discussed extensively is the question of the Holy Spirit's relationship to the interpretative process.

The term "hermeneutics" is generally understood to mean the art and science of interpreting and elucidating written materials. The term's origin is from the Greek *hermeneuein*, which means "to interpret."[1] Lewis S. Mudge, like others, believes that it is derived from the name of the Greek god Hermes, "the messenger of the gods who makes intelligible to human beings that which otherwise cannot be grasped."[2]

The need for hermeneutics grows particularly out of the problems encountered when attempting to understand difficult texts. When the materials being considered are from one's own time and culture, written in the reader's common language and dealing with a familiar subject, understanding may occur without special effort. The need for rules, methods, and theory arises when one is confronted with materials that are unfamiliar or strange for any reason. Ancient texts are difficult since

1. See Behm, "Hermeneuo," 661–62.

2. Mudge, "Hermeneutics," 250.

"gaps" such as the historical gap, the cultural gap, and the linguistic gap separate the reader from the material. Hermeneutics is the discipline that seeks to give guidance in understanding these writings.[3]

Hermeneutics as a discipline especially relates to the study of the Bible. Richard E. Palmer notes that "the word [hermeneutics] came into modern use precisely as the need arose for books setting forth the rules for proper exegesis of Scripture."[4] The Bible obviously consists of materials that are considered to be unfamiliar and strange to modern readers. The books of the Bible contain ancient writings produced centuries ago by authors living in varied cultures that were drastically different from present times. To understand the Scripture and find its meaning today, one must bridge several gaps such as those mentioned above.

If the issue had to do only with the basic hermeneutical question of how one properly understands an ancient text, the problem would be difficult enough. The fact that the text in question is an ancient text called "Scripture" makes the problem considerably more difficult. The religious subject matter of the Bible and the longstanding claims about it being special revelation automatically make the matter of understanding Scripture not only a hermeneutical question, but also a theological one. For some believe that, among ancient literature, the Bible has a certain distinctiveness. It is held to be a "religious" book—the "word of God" written for today. It is not just a literary product of past human genius, but also a "divine revelation" from God to modern humanity. Geoffrey W. Bromiley poses a pertinent question: "Is then a divine message to be abstracted from what is concretely said?" Answering in the affirmative, he says: "The divine Word is given through human words."[5]

Also, even those who deny that the Bible is special revelation and seek to understand its contents in the same manner as any other ancient text ultimately cannot completely avoid the theological nature of their activity. This is because basic hermeneutics acknowledges that any text "cannot be understood apart from a full recognition of the text's relationship to and focus on the matter which is discussed in it."[6] The "matter" that the Bible discusses is obviously theological. That is, this text claims

---

3. See Ramm, "Hermeneutics," 100.

4. Palmer, *Hermeneutics*, 283.

5. Bromiley, "The Interpretation of the Bible," 64.

6. Berkouwer, *Holy Scripture*, 115.

to discuss God and his relationship to humanity. Thus, biblical hermeneutics is from the beginning inherently a theological enterprise.

This distinctiveness pertaining to the nature of the Bible suggests at least the possibility of some correspondingly distinctive challenges in biblical hermeneutics. Bromiley writes: "With the difficulties it shares with other written statements, Scripture has some special hermeneutical difficulties of its own."[7] He and others believe that a unique "gap" exists for the reader who seeks to understand the biblical material and comprehend its ultimate message. Humanity, the fallen human creature, is attempting to understand not just an ordinary message from another human, but also a divine message from an unfamiliar, transcendent realm. Millard J. Erickson believes that the "ontological difference between God and man" complicates the interpretative process.[8] Some, then, contend that grammatically understanding the biblical material according to its ancient historical and cultural setting is only a part of the task. Beyond this is the task of understanding the divine "spiritual" or "religious" significance of Scripture.

The claim that the Bible is a "religious" book, the "word of God" written for today, thus indicates for some a unique intricacy in biblical hermeneutics. Ramm suggests that when it deals with Scripture, hermeneutics is a "theological discipline" that has as its goal not only exegesis but also exposition. The ultimate goal is not just to ascertain what the author said in the original historical context, but also to discover the meaning or significance of the Scripture text for the contemporary generation.[9] F. F. Bruce succinctly states the position that in biblical hermeneutics the endeavor is necessarily broadened to include an additional aspect or level. He says:

> For those who accept the Bible as sacred text, the church's book, the record of God's unique self-revelation, its interpretation cannot be conducted on the grammatico-historical level alone. That level is fundamental, but there is a theological level.[10]

Concerning interpretation of Scripture, John Breck notes: "Although based upon scientific procedure, it transcends the limits of pure science

---

7. Bromiley, "The Interpretation of the Bible," 63.

8. Erickson, *Christian Theology*, 247.

9. Ramm, "Hermeneutics," 100.

10. Bruce, "Interpretation of the Bible," 566.

to delve into the realm of divine mystery—a realm that by its very nature exists beyond the field of empirical research."[11]

Various questions are raised by the view that there are some unique challenges or difficulties pertaining to biblical hermeneutics. For example: If indeed the ontological difference between God and humanity presents a unique gap to the Bible reader, what is involved in bridging this gap? How is it accomplished? If there is a divine intent for Scripture that includes "spiritual" or "religious" aspects, what might be the role of the Holy Spirit in bringing this understanding to the reader? Must divine assistance be involved? If the Holy Spirit is involved, does he work in this special way with all readers or only with certain individuals? The focus of this study pertains to these and other questions.

Statement of the Problem

Succinctly stated, the problem to be examined is: In contemporary understanding, what, if any, is the relationship of the Holy Spirit to biblical hermeneutics? First, the aim of this study is to analyze the literature on hermeneutics to see what is said about the Holy Spirit's work in relation to it. The purpose is to present the views of past and present scholars on the relationship of the Holy Spirit to the interpretative process. Second, the aim is to synthesize these views and to explore the possibility of moving toward a clearer, more complete conceptualization of how the Holy Spirit may be involved. The main focus is hermeneutics with a special interest in discussing the relationship that the Holy Spirit may have to the process.

The proposed study seeks to answer these fundamental questions. What is the nature of historical precedence with regard to positing a role of the Holy Spirit in the interpretative process? Why do some scholars omit or deny a role of the Holy Spirit in hermeneutics? Why do some scholars conceive of the Spirit having a role in interpretation, and what is the ground of pneumatic involvement in the hermeneutical process? If the Holy Spirit is involved, what is the nature and content of knowledge gained as a result of this involvement? Who qualifies as a Spirit-guided interpreter; i.e., with whom does the Holy Spirit work in the process? How does the Holy Spirit work with the interpreter; what is the nature of the Spirit's role in relationship to that of the human interpreter? What

---

11. Breck, "Exegesis and Interpretation," 90–91.

model or models might be used to conceptualize in contemporary terms the role of the Holy Spirit in the hermeneutical process?

Definitions of Terms

When attempting to answer these questions and address the proposed problem, one soon encounters a significant difficulty with semantics. Important terms in the field of hermeneutics are commonly used in the literature with broad, vague, and varying connotations of meaning. These terms include: "hermeneutics," "exegesis," "exposition," "interpretation," and "meaning."

To understand the discussion and to recognize the nature of the issue at hand, the reader must know how scholars commonly use these terms. "Hermeneutics" is generally understood to mean the art and science of interpreting and elucidating difficult texts. It includes the theory, methods, and principles of the interpretative process. It begins with the discovery of the original meaning of the text (exegesis) and includes the elucidation of its message (exposition) for modern readers.[12] "Exegesis" is the process of bringing out of the text the meaning intended by the author and understood by the original readers in their historical situation. "Exposition" is the message that is relevant to contemporary times in light of current situations and in keeping with the original meaning of the text.[13] "Interpretation" may refer either to the meaning in the original historical situation when the text was written and/or the present relevant message of the text for modern readers.[14] The term "meaning" is variously used in the same general sense as the term "interpretation." Writers are often quite vague in their usage of these last two terms. The reader must attempt to recognize from the context how the writer intends for them to be understood.

The above definitions and descriptions of terms indicate the current usage. They help the reader understand the discussion in chapters 2 and 3. However, in chapters 4 and 5, where the discussion moves to-

---

12. Mudge, "Hermeneutics," 250; Also, note Bruce's broad, comprehensive definition in *EDT* 565: "The study of the principles of interpretation—both the grammaticohistorical interpretation and the practical application of that interpretation in the pulpit—is called hermeneutics."

13. Ramm, "Hermeneutics," 100–1;, Also, see Leschert, "Inspired Hermeneutics?" 48.

14. See Bruce, "Interpretation of the Bible," 565.

wards synthesizing a more comprehensive and precise articulation of the topic, attempt must be made to resolve the problem of semantics. Therefore, more precise definitions and usages of certain terms are suggested in the introduction of chapter 4. Thereafter, these terms are used more explicitly to refer to specific aspects of hermeneutics and the Holy Spirit's relationship to the process.

NEED FOR THE STUDY

Importance of the Study

Among both Protestant and Catholic scholars today, there is renewed awareness of the importance of hermeneutics. For example, Ramm states: "The Protestant ministry is based upon the Word of God as expressed in the inspired canonical literature." He adds: "The main concern in the right use of the Word of God is its proper interpretation."[15] Likewise, Catholic scholar Sandra M. Schneiders notes: "Catholics, for the first time in centuries, are vitally interested in the biblical bases for their faith and practice."[16] She represents scholars of this tradition who are dealing with hermeneutics in their search for "the contemporary meaning of the Bible."[17]

This renewed awareness of the importance of hermeneutics is also commonly accompanied by an interest in the Holy Spirit's relationship to the interpretative process. Discussions of this relationship are scattered throughout the literature. These discussions are, however, usually brief and lacking in both depth and breath.

Lack of Previous Studies

Previous studies dealing extensively with the issue of the Holy Spirit's relationship to hermeneutics are noticeably lacking. A search for dissertations, including a computer search of the Comprehensive Dissertation Index, reveals only dissertations that deal incidentally or indirectly with the topic.[18] Discussions of the Holy Spirit's relationship to the herme-

---

15. Ramm, "Hermeneutics," 99.

16. Schneiders, "Faith, Hermeneutics, and the Literal Sense of Scripture," 720.

17. Ibid., 725; see McKim, A Guide to Contemporary Hermeneutics, where the contributors represent scholarship from a range of Christian views.

18. Among the dissertations located, the two which are the most relevant to the

neutical process found in other unpublished materials and in journal articles, essays, and books are usually brief. Roy B. Zuck notes: "Biblical scholars have wrestled and are wrestling with serious hermeneutical issues but comparatively little attention has been given to the Holy Spirit's role in hermeneutics."[19]

This lack of attention to the Holy Spirit's role in hermeneutics is part of the larger problem of general neglect of pneumatology through the centuries. William Barclay suggests:

> It may well be said that the story of the Bible is the story of Spirit-filled men. And yet for the most part it remains true that our thinking about the Spirit is vaguer and more undefined than our thinking about any other part of the Christian Faith.[20]

Thus, Ian T. Ramsey, like others, is concerned about the confusion and over-simplification that result from neglect of pneumatology since the second century of the church. He observes: "The doctrine of the Holy Spirit, where above all places Christian discourse should come alive to make its point, seems particularly tangled and tortuous."[21] Wolfhart Pannenberg concurs:

> In the New Testament, Spirit is the name for the actual presence of divine reality in Christian experience and in the Christian community. Therefore, one might expect nothing to be more familiar to every Christian than the reality of the Spirit. But to the contrary, there is almost no other subject in modern theology so difficult to deal with as the doctrine of the Holy Spirit is. To begin with, it is rather hard to find out what kind of reality one is talking about in referring to the Holy Spirit.[22]

---

present study are: DeVenny, "The Holy Spirit as the Interpreter of the Old Testament in the New Testament Community"; and Watts, "The Theological Method of G. C. Berkouwer."

19. Zuck, "The Role of the Holy Spirit in Hermeneutics," 120; Also, see Klooster, "The Role of the Holy Spirit in the Hermeneutic Process," 451, where Klooster makes a similar observation.

20. Barclay, *The Promise of the Spirit*, 11.

21. Ramsey, *Models for Divine Activity*, 2. In this book, Ramsey seeks to answer the question: "What can we do to trace some pathways, logical and theological, through discourse about the Spirit?"

22. Pannenberg, "The Working of the Spirit in the Creation and in the People of God," 13.

The present study cannot concern itself with the broad extent of this larger problem. It does, however, propose to address a particular aspect of it; namely, the relationship of the Holy Spirit to biblical hermeneutics. There is a need for more extensive and detailed consideration of this matter. Carl F. H. Henry, in his discussion of "The Spirit as Divine Illuminator," notes: "Theologians of the past . . . left us no full delineation of the Holy Spirit's ministry." He regrets that even today "theologians can write volumes on the Bible with not even a single index reference to the Holy Spirit's work of illumination."[23] Stephen Neill likewise recognizes the "lack of a theology of the Holy Spirit, as the one through whom time and distance are annihilated, and through whom the Word of Jesus becomes the living and contemporary word."[24] Thus, the various views, conceptions, and models need to be brought together and analyzed in a systematic fashion. Areas of agreement may suggest a basic view of the Spirit's role in hermeneutics and provide a beginning ground for common affirmation. Points of disagreement may present a challenge to sharpen the focus on this important issue. Models suggested by various scholars may serve as paradigms for a broadened conception of the Holy Spirit's involvement in the interpretative process.

INVESTIGATION OF THE PROBLEM

Method

The methodology most predominately employed throughout is the descriptive and analytical techniques of research. The study also applies the historical method, especially in the second chapter where the historical background is set for understanding the contemporary situation. In the last two chapters, the synthetical technique is used in an attempt to develop further comprehension and articulation of the Holy Spirit's role in hermeneutics.

Since this study is largely an exercise in philosophical theology, consideration of models will be especially useful. Ian G. Barbour describes models as "imagined mental constructs invented to account for observed phenomena."[25] Max Black suggests: "All intellectual pursuits, however

23. Henry, *God Who Speaks and Shows*, 256, 272–73.

24. Neill, *The Interpretation of the New Testament: 1861–1961*, 235.

25. Barbour, *Myths, Models, and Paradigms*, 16.

different their aims and methods, rely firmly upon such exercises of the imagination."[26] Especially relevant to this study, Avery Dulles notes:

> Theological models are for religion, in an analogous way, what theoretical models are for science. Their purpose is . . . to suggest ways of accounting for theologically relevant data and for explaining, up to a point, what Christians believe on a motive of faith.[27]

Ramsey lists three ways in which models help theologians to be articulate. One, models are "builders of discourse, . . . giving rise to large-scale interpretations of phenomena that so far lack a theological mapping." Two, models "enable us to make sense of discourse whose logical structure is so perplexing as to inhibit literacy." Three, models "enable us to talk of what eludes us."[28]

The present writer is aware of the possible dangers and limitations of the use of models. Models are like a two-edged sword. That which makes them valuable to the user also gives them inherent possibility of being detrimental. In using models, one moves from the concrete to the abstract, from the actual to the ideal and from the particular to the universal. Therefore, models do not give a literal picture of reality. They tend towards oversimplification; and they cannot prove the truth they suggest.

Models are nevertheless valuable tools. These dangers and limitations must only be noted and guarded against. They must not prevent theologians from using models. Dulles says: "The fact that [models] fail to represent the reality literally and comprehensively does not deprive them of cognitive value." He sees models as useful instruments in developing theories that in some sense explain certain phenomena. Models suggest possible ways of thinking consistently about certain problems and assist in deriving ways of accounting for theologically relevant data.[29] "Models, in essences, are expectancies," Morris L. Bigge says. They enable the one who uses them to take the information given and go beyond to new understandings.[30]

---

26. Black, *Models and Metaphors*, 242.

27. Dulles, *Models of Revelation*, 32.

28. Ramsey, *Models and Mystery*, 14–15.

29. Dulles, *Models of Revelation*, 31–32

30. Bigge, *Learning Theories for Teachers*, 250.

The use of models is especially relevant to the enterprise of theology. Theology deals with the mysteries of faith. Models—with their adeptness to move from the concrete to the abstract, from the actual to the ideal, and from the specific to the general—are highly functional in probing the mysteries of the divine being and the divine activity. Dulles says: "Theological systems, with the help of theoretical models, illuminate certain aspects of a reality too complex and exalted for human comprehension."[31] By theorizing with models, theologians aid humanity in understanding a mysterious universe.[32] Thus, in considering the issue of the Holy Spirit's role in hermeneutics, this research will be looking for promising models "with implications rich enough to suggest novel hypotheses and speculations."[33]

Scope

The proposed study focuses on those concepts and issues that are considered to be central and decisive to the question of the Holy Spirit's relationship to biblical hermeneutics in contemporary understanding. The scope of the historical section is limited. This is in keeping with its primary purpose of supplying a brief developmental background for a better understanding of contemporary views. Complete coverage of either of the broader areas—the Holy Spirit's work in revelation or hermeneutical theory—is beyond the scope of this inquiry. Rather, both of these are treated only as they have bearing on the central focus of this investigation.

The central focus of this study is the question of the Holy Spirit's role in biblical hermeneutics. Basically, there are two possible positions. One, "No, he does not play a role." Two, "Yes, he does play a role." Logically, one's answer is directly related to his or her concept of the Bible as special revelation. On the one hand, if one does not view the Bible as being God's special revelation, then correspondingly he or she would not likely conceive of there being any divine activity—identified as the Holy Spirit—associated with understanding it. In that case, a role of the Holy Spirit in hermeneutics would be a moot issue. Hermeneutical approaches that do not consider the Bible to be special revelation are there-

---

31. Dulles, *Models of Revelation*, 32.

32. Ramsey, *Models and Mystery*, 20 (emphasis mine).

33. Black, *Models and Metaphors*, 233.

fore beyond the scope of this inquiry. On the other hand, if one does view the Bible as being God's special revelation to humanity—a revelation that has relevance to contemporary times, then two possibilities follow. One, the Bible is special revelation to humanity; but contemporary men and women are capable of understanding it by their ordinary senses and normal reasoning abilities. In that case, the reader can discover anything there is to understand in Scripture without special assistance from the Spirit. Two, the Bible is a special revelation of God to humanity; and presently the Holy Spirit is active, in some manner, in assisting human beings to understand Scripture and its contemporary significance. These two possibilities and their attending issues comprise the purview of this inquiry.

The scope of this study also includes arguments and models that render a positive affirmation of the Holy Spirit's role in hermeneutics as plausible, though not necessarily as provable. This aspect allows the investigation to move beyond an initial negative denial or a simple positive affirmation. Other attending issues can thus be discussed more adequately. Such an exercise in philosophical theology allows for a move towards further reflection on the subject of the Holy Spirit's relationship to biblical hermeneutics.

ORGANIZATION OF THE STUDY

The dissertation is organized into five chapters. The first chapter introduces the study. The second chapter presents a brief historical analysis of the subject and related areas. This provides background necessary for a better understanding of the issue in the current situation. The third chapter examines the issues raised and the positions taken by contemporary scholars. This part of the study reveals various models. The fourth chapter discusses methodology for more fully understanding the Holy Spirit's relationship to hermeneutics. A model is proposed for picturing the Holy Spirit's role, the reader's role, and the expected results when the Holy Spirit is a participant in the process. The fifth chapter consists of conclusions derived from the material presented in the earlier chapters and includes suggested areas for further investigation of the subject.

2

Historical Background

INTRODUCTION

THIS STUDY BEGINS WITH a brief historical analysis of the church's views and practices related to biblical interpretation. The issues underlying the question of the Holy Spirit's relationship to hermeneutics can best be understood and discussed when one is aware of past developments in areas such as the doctrine of Scripture, hermeneutics, pneumatology, and related areas. Gerhard Hasel notes: "The present has its roots in the past and cannot be adequately understood without a knowledge of it."[1]

Church history can be divided severally into various periods, depending upon the nature and purpose of a given study. In the history of biblical hermeneutics from the Early Church to the present, two epochs provided circumstances that produced major turning points in the interpretation of Scripture. These epochs were the Reformation and the Enlightenment. Thus, the history of the church's interpretation of Scripture divides naturally into three periods: Early Church to Reformation; Reformation to Enlightenment; and Enlightenment to mid-twentieth century.

In each of these three periods, selected representative individuals are sufficient to show the development of hermeneutical principles and practices as they relate to the question of the Holy Spirit's role. These principles and practices grow out of the interpreters' view of the nature of the Bible, their understanding of the Holy Spirit's relationship to Scripture, and their positions concerning certain other philosophical and theological issues.

---

1. Hasel, *New Testament Theology*, 11, 12.

EARLY CHURCH TO REFORMATION

Following the first century, the Christian Fathers responded to the need to make the Scripture's message understandable and applicable to new situations in various regions of the world. The history of interpretation is the history of the church's efforts to adjust to new cultural settings and respond to questions about its message. At first no prevalent approach or approaches emerged to leave any lasting imprints. Eventually, however, from the second century forward, certain approaches and methods developed into significant trends if not identifiable "schools" of interpretation. The first schools or trends of influence which successively arose to dominance over lesser received approaches and methods included: the Alexandrian school; the Antiochian school; the Latin influence; and the Scholastic influence.[2]

Alexandrian School

The Alexandrian school had its center of origin during the second century in the Christian community in North Africa. It continued until near the end of the fourth century. Its first teacher was Pantaenus. Clement of Alexandria was his successor, but Origen (185–254) was "the greatest master of this school."[3] Origen clearly established himself as its definitive representative.

Like other interpreters, Origen's method was largely influenced by his view of Scripture. He shared a view of Scripture common to Christians of Alexandrian and elsewhere at that time. For Origen the Bible was authoritative because "the sacred Scriptures were not composed by any human words but were written by the inspiration of the Holy Spirit."[4] This "divine inspiration of holy Scripture," he said, "extends throughout its body."[5] The entire Bible was equally authoritative.

The close relationship of the Holy Spirit to the writing of the Scripture was foundational to Origen's ideas and practices of interpretation. First, he emphasized the "spiritual" meaning of Scripture. He

2. Farrar, *History of Interpretation*, 182–272.

3. Ibid., 183, 187.

4. Origen, *An Exhortation to Martyrdom, On Prayer, On First Principles*: Book IV, *The Prologue to the Commentary on The Song of Songs, Homily XXVII on Numbers*, 180.

5. Origen, "De Principiis," 355.

conceived that "just as a human being is said to be made up of body, soul, and spirit, so also is sacred Scripture."[6] Therefore, the Scripture had three senses: the literal; the moral; and the spiritual. Since the spiritual sense was regarded as the most important of these, he gave most of his attention to it. Allegorizing, for which the Alexandrian school was especially noted, was Origen's chief method of understanding this deeper and often hidden spiritual truth.[7]

Second, just as the Holy Spirit participated in the writing of Scripture, he also participated in its interpretation. In explaining "the right way of understanding Scripture," Origen stated: "it is the Holy Spirit's purpose to enlighten holy souls" and to turn "the mind of the reader to the examination of the inner meaning." Like the writers of Scripture, an interpreter needed to be "taught by the Spirit" (1 Cor. 2:12–13) and thereby to be "an ally of the Spirit's knowledge and a participant in the divine counsel." As interpreters, Origen said, "we ought . . . to turn the eyes of our mind toward him who ordered this to be written and to ask of him their meaning."[8]

Frederic Farrar concluded: "The influence of Origen was wide and deep."[9] Jack Rogers and Donald McKim noted: "It was Origen who laid the foundation and built much of the framework of later biblical interpretation."[10] This influence and foundation included a definite role of the Holy Spirit not only in the writing of Scripture, but also in its interpretation.

Antiochian School

The next significant influence in biblical interpretation arose in Antioch of Syria. Beginning with Theophilus in the middle of the second century, the Antiochian school vied with the Alexandrian school in the West for dominance.[11] Antioch gained pre-eminence in the latter quarter of the fourth century, under the leadership of Diodorus of Tarsus. "The

6. Origen, *On First Principles*, 182.

7. Mickelsen, *Interpreting the Bible*, 32. See Origen, *On First Principles*, 188, where Origen explained that the Holy Spirit had interwoven the narrative of Scripture with spiritual meaning, "hiding the secret meaning more deeply."

8. Origen, *On First Principles*, 180–88, 247.

9. Farrar, *History of Interpretation*, 201

10. Rogers and McKim, *The Authority and Interpretation of the Bible*, 11.

11. Grant and Tracy, *A Short History of the Interpretation of the Bible*, 63, 84.

'bright consummate flower' of the school of Antioch," however, was John Chrysostom (354–407).[12]

Chrysostom agreed with the Alexandrian school in maintaining the divine inspiration and authority of Scripture. He held the Bible in the highest esteem and reverence because to him it was "simply the holy and infallible word of God."[13] Chrysostom differed, however, from the Alexandrian school in his method of interpretation. In theory, he recognized the allegorizing method of Origen, but Chrysostom seldom practiced it. He strongly favored the literal sense instead. He sought to explain the obvious grammatical and historical meaning of the text.[14]

Like Origen, Chrysostom saw a close association of the Holy Spirit with the Bible. The Holy Spirit, he said, was the one who knew the secret things of God, and he was the one who conveyed them to us in the Scriptures.[15] The following passage from his second homily on Saint John indicates that Chrysostom saw the writing of Scripture to be a cooperative activity involving the human writer and the Holy Spirit:

> Were John about . . . to say to us words of his own, we needs must describe his family, his country, and his education. But since it is not he, but God by him, that speaks to mankind, it seems to me superfluous and distracting to enquire into these matters. And yet even thus it is not superfluous, but even very necessary. For when you have learned who he was, and from whence, who his parents, and what his character, and then hear his voice and all his heavenly wisdom, then you shall know right well that these (doctrines) belong not to him, but to the Divine power stirring his soul.[16]

Also, according to Chrysostom, the Holy Spirit not only inspired the authors to write Scriptures, he also made "many wise provisions in order that they might be safely kept" for us.[17]

Chrysostom indicated he believed the involvement of the Holy Spirit was also needed in the task of understanding Scripture. The Spirit

---

12. Farrar, *History of Interpretation*, 210–20.

13. Baur, *John Chrysostom and His Times*, 318.

14. Schaff, "Prolegomena" to *Saint Chrysostom*, 18.

15. Chrysostom, *Homilies on the Epistles of Paul to the Corinthians*, 36–37.

16. Chrysostom, *Homilies on the Gospel of Saint John, Part I*, 9.

17. Chrysostom, *Homilies on the Gospel of St. John and the Epistle to the Hebrews*, 407.

was "the Comforter, the Omnipresent, who knoweth the things of God, . . . the guiding Spirit," Who gave men eyes, "fitting them to see things."[18] As in the case of the writing of Scripture, Chrysostom saw interpretation as a cooperative effort. When looking into "the depth of the Divine Scriptures," he said, "it is not possible to discover their meaning in a careless way, . . . but there needs close search, and there needs earnest prayer, that we may be enabled to see . . . into the secrets of the divine oracles."[19] Thus, he considered the Spirit to be the reader's needed master Teacher.[20] Geoffrey Bromiley noted: "Chrysostom pleaded for faith in the reading of Scripture so that one may hear the voice of the Spirit and thus be enabled to perceive heavenly things."[21]

Latin Influence

Even while Chrysostom was clarifying and establishing the position of the Antiochian school, the Latin Fathers were beginning to bring significant influence to bear upon biblical studies in the West. Jerome (347–419) became renown not only as a translator (the Latin Vulgate) but also as a biblical exegete. Farrar observed, however, that Jerome was often both hasty and indecisive in biblical interpretation.[22] Clarity and firmness of the Latin influence was provided by Augustine (354–430) who, in his work entitled *On Christian Doctrine*, produced "the earliest manual of Biblical hermeneutics."[23]

Augustine wrote often of his conviction concerning "the authority of the holy writings." He observed that the more he studied the Bible "its authority seemed . . . all the more venerable and worthy."[24] His admonition was: "Let us therefore give in and yield our assent to the authority of Holy Scripture, which knows not how either to be deceived or to deceive."[25]

18. Chrysostom, *Homilies on the Gospel of Saint John, Part I*, 4.

19. Ibid., 173.

20. Chrysostom, *Homilies on the Epistles of Paul to the Corinthians*, 37.

21. Bromiley, "The Church Fathers and Holy Scripture," 214.

22. Farrar, *History of Interpretation*, 222–28.

23. Schaff, *A Select Library of the Nicene and Post-Nicene Fathers of the Christian Church*, x.

24. Augustin, *The Confessions*, 93.

25. Augustin, *Anti-Pelagian Writings*, 28.

Augustine related the authority of Scripture to a doctrine of inspiration. He "rarely tried to prove the inspiration of the Bible. He took the inspiration for granted because of the effect the Bible had on people."[26] Polman noted that Augustine variously attributed inspiration to God, to Christ, and to the Holy Spirit. This was in keeping with his belief that all the external works of the Trinity were indivisible.[27] Yet Augustine occasionally specified the Holy Spirit as the source of Scripture. He argued for the belief: "Scriptures were imparted unto mankind by the Spirit."[28] In commenting on some of Paul's writings, Augustine said, "the Apostle, nay rather the Spirit of God" was therein exhorting the readers.[29]

Augustine believed that in the activity of providing Scripture, God condescended to accommodate these writings to the limited capacity of the human mind. He wrote: "Holy Scripture . . . suits itself to babes . . . [in order that] as by nourishment, our understanding might rise gradually to things divine and transcendent."[30] Thus, the reader could safely follow the Scripture, which proceeded at a pace like a mother leading her child, and not be left behind in weakness.[31]

Accommodation did not mean, however, that the meaning of all Scripture was always obviously clear and that interpretation was easy in all cases. Polman summarized Augustine's thoughts on the perspicuity of Scripture as follows: "Scripture is clear and obscure, simple and profound, lucid and yet full of mysteries, sometimes so plain one can grasp its meaning even in one's sleep, then again so deep that no man can fully plumb its depths." Polman observed that for Augustine, Scripture was "quite clear about all things needful for obtaining salvation and for living a godly life." Yet beyond that there remained "many mysteries" to be inquired into by those who were advancing in the study of Scripture.[32]

Augustine reached a balanced view between the need for diligent effort by the interpreter and reliance on the Holy Spirit. In his "Preface" to *On Christian Doctrine*, Augustine denied that God "communicated everything that he wished to be taught to men by voices from heaven."

26. Rogers and McKim, *Authority and Interpretation of the Bible*, 25–26.

27. Polman, *The Word of God According to St. Augustine*, 44.

28. Augustine, *Confessions*, 93.

29. Augustine, *Of the Work of Monks*, 513.

30. Ibid., 18.

31. Rogers and McKim, *Authority and Interpretation of the Bible*, 27.

32. Polman, *Word of God According to St. Augustine*, 66–69.

He scorned Christians who claimed a special "inward teaching of the Spirit" and those who professed "to understand the Scriptures without any direction from man." He claimed rather that the rules for interpretation, which he was about to state, were necessary. If one would read them and hold fast to them he or she would be able to understand obscure passages properly.[33]

Augustine also believed that the Holy Spirit was "at work in the present-day reading of Scripture," and his assistance was necessary for its illumination.[34] "Often, when he had to interpret a difficult Biblical passage, he would say that he could only perform that task in so far as the Lord or the Holy Ghost would inspire him."[35] Before presenting his rules for the interpretation of Scripture, Augustine declared that such a task must "be undertaken in dependence on God's aid." He said: "Presumptuous it would undoubtedly be, if I were counting on my own strength."[36]

Scholastic Influence

Following the time of Augustine, the world entered a transition period into the Middle Ages. During this transition one of the most significant shifts was the change from the Platonic-based to Aristotelian-based approach to Scripture. Augustine lived in a world dominated by Platonism. Therefore, theologically, he believed understanding was primarily the fruit of faith. Reason could help one in the quest for full understanding of the transcendent truths of God; but for Augustine, faith always preceded reason. By the thirteenth century, however, the shift was made to an Aristotelian-based theology and approach to Scripture. Significantly, in this approach, reason came before faith in gaining understanding.[37]

This epistemological shift to the priority of reason was central to what became known as "scholasticism," a term used to describe the medieval approach to the liberal arts, philosophy, and theology. This approach developed a four-step method: question, tentative answer, reconsideration, and definitive answer. John Scotus Erigena (ca. 815–877) was a forerunner to this movement with his view that reason, illumi-

---

33. Augustine, *City of God* and *On Christian Doctrine*, 520–21.

34. Rogers and McKim, *Authority and Interpretation of the Bible*, 26.

35. Polman, *Word of God According to St. Augustine*, 45.

36. Augustine, *On Christian Doctrine*, 522.

37. Rogers and McKim, *Authority and Interpretation of the Bible*, 23–25, 43–44.

nated by God, could investigate and explain the biblical data. Anselm (ca. 1033–1109) believed he could rely on human reason to appeal to an open-minded nonbeliever to move toward faith. Abelard (1079–1142) advanced on the views of Erigena and Anselm, but Thomas Aquinas (ca. 1225–1274) was the theologian who fully "incorporated the Aristotelian scheme . . . and brought it to theological expression in a comprehensive system."[38]

Farrar rated Aquinas "profound as a thinker, incomparable as a theologian, [but] least successful in the interpretation of Scripture." Negatively he asked: "How much has any reader really added to his understanding of the Scriptures" when he has read after Aquinas.[39] Grant agreed when he noted that Aquinas and the other medieval theologians added little that was strikingly novel in biblical interpretation.[40]

Farrar's and Grant's evaluations were based upon their observation that Aquinas' view of Scripture and his practices of interpretation appeared to be much like those discussed above. He believed that God was "the author of holy Scripture." Therefore, the Bible was authoritative for all Christians.[41] Although he accepted Origen's allegorical method, he favored Chrysostom's approach. In their study, Rogers and McKim concluded that Aquinas, like Chrysostom, turned attention away from allegorical speculation to grammatico-historical interpretation and the literal sense.[42]

Nevertheless, Aquinas in fact exerted a significant influence on biblical interpretation. This was the case for two reasons. One, he did more than just emphasize grammatical-historical interpretation. He strongly insisted that all meanings are based on one, namely the literal sense. He wrote: "From this [literal sense] alone can arguments be drawn, . . . nothing necessary for faith is contained under the spiritual sense that is not openly conveyed through the literal sense."[43] Two, Aquinas placed reason in priority over faith. His position "that all knowledge begins in human sense impressions reversed the Augustinian priority of faith over

38. Ibid., 36–44.

39. Farrar, *History of Interpretation*, 269, 271.

40. Grant and Tracy, *Short History of the Interpretation of the Bible*, 83.

41. Aquinas, *The Existence of God*, 59.

42. Rogers and McKim, *Authority and Interpretation of the Bible*, 47.

43. Aquinas, *The Existence of God*, 60.

reason. Reason now came first."[44] This new approach was quite important for it significantly impacted his view of interpretation. For Aquinas, reason, by giving understanding of the literal sense, "openly conveyed" any spiritual sense to be found in Scripture. Therefore, the interpretation of Scripture required no special inner grace. Rather than depending on the Holy Spirit illuminating the mind as Augustine did, Aquinas relied on the power of reason appealing to the mind.[45]

Aquinas' scholastic approach was more rationalistic than either the Fathers before him or the Reformers after him.[46] It "represented a movement away from the early church's common foundations of theological method and its approach to the Bible." While this movement's influence upon interpretation was greatly diminished by the Reformation, scholastic tendencies continued in some circles. Scholasticism was developed especially by Francis Turretin during the Post-Reformation era. Following the Enlightenment it greatly impacted the Princeton Seminarians' view of and approach to Scripture.[47]

Summary

From the first centuries of the church, the Fathers held a view of inspiration that made Scripture authoritative for doctrine. They developed a variety of principles and practices that guided them in interpretation. Invariably they looked for a "spiritual" meaning in the text. Their methods of finding that meaning varied from Origen's allegorization to Aquinas' scholasticism. Except for Aquinas, they stressed that the Holy Spirit played a necessary role in aiding the interpreter to understand Scripture. After Origen, interpreters generally followed the lead of the Antiochian school. Thus, a grammatical-historical emphasis was included along with the "spiritual" approach, giving a balance to the hermeneutical process.

---

44. Rogers and McKim, *Authority and Interpretation of the Bible*, 43, 46.

45. Ibid., 40, 44–46.

46. Grant and Tracy, *Short History of the Interpretation of the Bible*, 91.

47. Rogers and McKim, *Authority and Interpretation of the Bible*, 37, 172–76, 265–310.

REFORMATION TO ENLIGHTENMENT

By the end of Aquinas' career the Renaissance was already beginning to provide the setting for significant new developments in biblical interpretation. Renewed interest in learning in general was accompanied by new awareness of and regard for Scripture. Louis Berkhof noted: "The Renaissance was of great importance for the development of sound Hermeneutical principles."[48]

The Renaissance was the backdrop for the Protestant Reformation whose battle cry was not only *sola gratia, sola fide*, but also *sola Scriptura*. A new understanding of Scripture arose with the rediscovery of the doctrine that justification is only through grace and by faith.[49] The Reformers regarded the Bible as the highest authority, and as the final court of appeal in all theological disputes. Over against the infallibility of the church they placed the infallibility of the Word.[50]

This shift in the locus of final authority was necessarily accompanied by renewed concern for clear and accurate interpretation of Scripture. If the church were not to determine what Scripture teaches, but rather Scripture was to determine what the church ought to teach; then, proper interpretation of Scripture was of utmost importance. This emphasis molded biblical interpretation throughout the Reformation and Post-Reformation era. The varied details of hermeneutics during this period were developed and refined by the early Continental Reformation, Reformed Scholasticism, and the English Reformation.

Early Continental Reformation

From the beginning of the Reformation period "the starting point for establishing exegetical principles was the new knowledge of the Word of God and of the exclusive authority of sacred scripture."[51] In response to this understanding and conviction, "the expositors of the Reformation . . . made a greater advance in the interpretation of Scripture than had been made during many previous centuries."[52] This advance, which

---

48. Berkhof, *Principles of Biblical Interpretation*, 25.

49. Runia, "The Hermeneutics of the Reformers," 122.

50. Berkhof, *Principles of Biblical Interpretation*, 26.

51. Kraus, "Calvin's Exegetical Principles," 9.

52. Farrar, *History of Interpretation*, 352.

Raymond Shelton called a "hermeneutical revolution,"[53] began early in the fifteenth century and set the tone and direction for biblical interpretation throughout the Reformation. The cumulative hermeneutic which grew out of the Reformation principle—*sola gratia, sola fide, sola scriptura*—became the most significant influence upon biblical studies until rationalism and the Age of Enlightenment.

Martin Luther (1483–1546) and John Calvin (1509–1564) were the primary leaders who gave definition to Reformation hermeneutics.[54] Luther was the principal figure who first set forth the Reformation principles. He likewise was the principal figure who began the accompanying hermeneutical advance. That advance began with an emphasis on the authority of Scripture and moved on to other principles and accompanying rules.[55]

Besides the doctrine of the supreme and final authority of Scripture, Luther also maintained other basic principles. These included: the sufficiency of Scripture; the priority of the literal sense of Scripture; the perspicuity of Scripture; and the privilege of every Christian to interpret and understand Scripture. Farrar discussed these principles and also listed Luther's primary rules of biblical interpretation. Luther insisted:

> (1) on the necessity for grammatical knowledge; (2) on the importance of taking into consideration times, circumstances, and conditions; (3) on the observance of the context; (4) on the need of faith and spiritual illumination; (5) on keeping what he called "the proportion of faith"; and (6) on the reference of all Scripture to Christ.[56]

With these principles and rules Luther united an "Augustinian acceptance of the Bible in faith, and a scholarly and critical appraisal of the natural, grammatical sense of the biblical text in its historical context." Contrary to Aquinas, Luther, like Augustine, put faith before reason; but "reason did have a legitimate place in the life of the believer when it

---

53. Shelton, "Martin Luther's Concept of Biblical Interpretation in Historical Perspective," 118.

54. This is not to say that others like Melanchthon and Zwingli did not make a contribution, but their uniqueness does not have special significance to this study. Farrar, in *History of Interpretation*, 341, said Zwingli "arrived at opinions on this subject [interpretation] which in all essential particulars coincided with those of Luther."

55. Shelton, "Martin Luther's Concept of Biblical Interpretation," 118.

56. Farrar, *History of Interpretation*, 332.

came after faith and was regenerated by the Holy Spirit." In the study of Scripture, "regenerated reason served to heighten Christian understanding that proceeded from faith." Thus, Luther could place a strong emphasis upon the historical and grammatical sense while also insisting upon the necessity of trusting the Holy Spirit's guidance. "Faith was the beginning and basis of sound theology, and careful study was the means of growing into Christian maturity."[57]

Putting faith before reason, Luther believed that competence in languages and history was not in itself sufficiently adequate to interpret Scripture. He held that for genuine depth of spiritual meaning one must experience the illumination of the Holy Spirit. Apart from this illumination, the interpreter would have only words and phrases.[58]

On the one hand, Luther suggested that when one began with prayer, God in his great mercy granted true understanding. On the other hand, some persons did not rightly understand the Bible because they approached Scripture only with reason—without faith. Consequently, they saw only the words of Scripture. Therefore, Luther said, although they "boast that they are teachers and experts in the Scriptures, they never speak justice or wisdom. For . . . they do not understand it. They are deceived by the outward fact that they cite the words of Scripture."[59] In Luther's conception, the Holy Spirit who inspired the Word also assisted the reader in comprehending it; and this guidance of the Spirit was essential to correct interpretation.[60]

Luther often spoke of the role of the Holy Spirit in bringing understanding of Scripture. Commenting on Ps 68:14 and John 10:3, he said: "the gatekeeper, the Holy Spirit, will open the door to those that enter. For if God does not open and explain Holy Writ, no one can understand it; it will remain a closed book, enveloped in darkness."[61] Discussing the task of understanding the truth of God's Word, he wrote: "No man can accept it unless his heart has been touched and opened by the Holy Spirit. It is as impossible of comprehension by reason as it is inaccessible

---

57. Rogers and McKim, *Authority and Interpretation of the Bible*, 76–83.

58. Mickelsen, *Interpreting the Bible*, 39.

59. Luther, *Selected Psalms III*, 223–24.

60. Shelton, "Martin Luther's Concept of Biblical Interpretation," 220–22.

61. Luther, *Selected Psalms II*, 16–17; Luther, *Sermons on the Gospel of St. John, Chapters 1–4*, 8.

to the touch of the hand." In his sermons on the Gospel of John, Luther counseled:

> If we want to find spirit and life, we . . . must become spiritual and hear the Word of God. This excels reason and rises higher than reason can rise. Any understanding of these words [of Scripture] that I hear must be wrought in me by the Holy Spirit.[62]

One should remember that Luther's emphasis upon the need for the Holy Spirit's assistance in understanding Scripture was balanced by other important complementary points. Luther, like the other Reformers, "insisted on an historical, literal, grammatical understanding of the Bible."[63] He often repudiated the traditional practice of allegorizing the text and, instead, stressed the objective elements in interpretation. Proper grammatical-historical and contextual understanding were not contrary to, but rather helpful to "spiritual" understanding.[64] While explaining a passage in Genesis, for example, Luther remarked: "You should be reminded of the historical facts, which serve in an excellent way to bring about a correct understanding of Scripture."[65] Charles Wood noted: "For Luther, there was not a spiritual sense in addition to a valid literal sense in a scriptural text; rather, the spiritual sense was the literal sense correctly understood."[66] Thus, while Luther began with faith and expected the assistance of the Holy Spirit, he also realized the need for human effort. He insisted on the interpreter engaging in "a scholarly and critical appraisal of the natural, grammatical sense of the biblical text in its historical context."[67]

Luther's emphasis upon the role of the Holy Spirit in interpretation was also balanced, or complemented, by his view of the relationship between revelation and Scripture. Luther adopted the Augustinian view regarding the "external Word" and the "internal Word." Scripture was the outward or external Word, and the voice of the Spirit was the inward or internal Word. In Luther's view, these two were closely related. In fact, the Spirit did not speak without the external Word; the Spirit

---

62. Luther, *Sermons on the Gospel of St. John, Chapters 6–8*, 175.

63. Grant and Tracy, *Short History of the Interpretation of the Bible*, 92–93.

64. Shelton, "Martin Luther's Concept of Biblical Interpretation," 223–24.

65. Luther, *Lectures on Genesis, Chapters 15–20*, 319.

66. Wood, "Finding the Life of a Text," 102.

67. Rogers and McKim, *Authority and Interpretation of the Bible*, 76; also, see Farrar, *History of Interpretation*, 332.

spoke only in and through the external Word. Thus, Luther firmly denied the Enthusiasts' belief that the Spirit gave new revelations separate from the Scripture. For Luther, there were no new revelations. The Holy Spirit spoke only through the Scripture.[68] He spoke strongly against the Enthusiasts who interpreted and twisted the Scripture "according to their pleasure."[69]

Further, Luther's emphasis upon the role of the Holy Spirit in interpretation was complemented by his insistence upon the position that all Christians can interpret and understand the Bible. Illumination of the Holy Spirit was not an elitist activity reserved for a few. Luther "indignantly swept aside the fiction of a usurping hierarchy, that priests were in any sense the sole authorized interpreters of Scripture." He firmly denied any "distinction between the spiritual capacity of the laity and the clergy." Rather, "he held that the Holy Spirit was given to all Christians, and therefore that the laity had a higher function than merely to register the decrees and interpretations of a ministerial class."[70]

In summary, Luther's emphasis upon Scripture as the final authority led to a more serious consideration of biblical interpretation. Correct understanding began with scholarly discovery of the historical and grammatical sense. With prayer, this was accompanied by the illuminating influence of the Holy Spirit—without which the reader could not gain an adequate understanding of Scripture. Thus, Luther "balanced the literal or grammatical sense with the spiritual depth of meaning."[71]

Calvin (1509–1564), who led the Swiss phase of the Reformation, held basically the same views of Scripture and principles of interpretation as those of Luther. Like Luther, Calvin adopted the traditional doctrine that Scripture had been given by the inspiration of the Holy Spirit, and he spoke "incessantly of the supreme and final authority of Scripture."[72] Kraus, who identified and discussed "eight exegetical principles . . . de-

---

68. Shelton, "Martin Luther's Concept of Biblical Interpretation," 240–42.

69. Runia, "Hermeneutics of the Reformers," 134–35. Enthusiasts included the Anabaptists who "claimed direct personal revelations from the Holy Spirit." Rogers and McKim, *Authority and Interpretation of the Bible*, 208.

70. Farrar, *History of Interpretation*, 330.

71. Mickelsen, *Interpreting the Bible*, 39.

72. Farrar, *History of Interpretation*, 349.

rived from Calvin's works," concluded that Calvin had "carefully studied and identified the various methods of interpretation used by Luther."[73]

Calvin, though, certainly was not an exact prototype of Luther. Klaas Runia suggested that Calvin, "as the more systematic thinker, amplified the new exegetical insights" pioneered by Luther.[74] Consequently, in keeping with his emphasis upon the authority of Scripture, Calvin established himself not just as a theologian, but foremost as a biblical interpreter.[75]

Calvin's interpretative practices grew out of his doctrine of Scripture—especially his view of the Spirit's relationship to the Scripture. Leon Allison observed: "One of the most vivid impressions that one gets from a study of Calvin's doctrine of Scripture is that most of what the author said on the subject centered upon the relationship of the Spirit and the Scripture."[76] John Murray thus called Calvin "the theologian of the Holy Spirit."[77]

Several important points were associated with Calvin's doctrine of the Spirit's relationship to Scripture. First, God's special revelation originated with the Spirit. The "light of truth" was given "exclusively" by God's Spirit who expressed this truth in the Scriptures. Thus, "by the light of the Spirit we are enabled therein to behold the Divine countenance."[78]

Second, Calvin especially emphasized that readers could be persuaded that Scripture was the Word of God only by the internal testimony of the Holy Spirit (*testimonium Spiritus Sancti internum*).[79] He wrote:

> The testimony of the Spirit is superior to all reason. For as God alone is a sufficient witness of himself in his own word, so also the word will never gain credit in the hearts of men, till it be confirmed by the internal testimony of the Spirit.[80]

73. Kraus, "Calvin's Exegetical Principles," 8, 12.

74. Runia, "Hermeneutics of the Reformers," 140, 142.

75. Mickelsen, *Interpreting the Bible*, 39. Also, see Berkhof, *Principles of Biblical Interpretation*, 27.

76. Allison, "The Doctrine of Scripture in the Theology of John Calvin and Francis Turretin," 17.

77. Murray, *Calvin as Theologian and Expositor*, 10.

78. Calvin, *Institutes of the Christian Religion*, 1:108–9.

79. Rogers and McKim, *Authority and Interpretation of the Bible*, 102–4.

80. Calvin, *Institutes*, 1:90.

This famous doctrine of illumination (*illuminatus*) was one of Calvin's most elaborated teachings because he believed it was "the final and definitive proof" that Scripture was from God himself.[81] Calvin thereby established himself firmly in the Platonic-Augustinian tradition of placing faith before reason.[82]

A third important point associated with Calvin's doctrine of the Spirit's relationship to the Scripture was that interpretation was also the work of the Spirit. Calvin taught that in illumination the Holy Spirit did much more than just confirm the authenticity of Scripture. H. Jackson Forstman found that for Calvin illumination also included the giving of understanding. "The Spirit must do more than confirm the scripture; it must 'illuminate the understanding (*illustrare mentes*)' in order that we may know the meaning of that which we know to be the word of God."[83]

Calvin wrote often in various contexts of the Holy Spirit illuminating the Scripture. For example, in his commentary on 1 Corinthians he wrote: "The Spirit of God . . . is its only true interpreter, to open it up to us." He also added: "Men's minds must of necessity be in blindness until they are enlightened by the Spirit of God."[84] In his commentary on 2 Peter he cautioned: "We ought not to rush on headlong and rashly when we read Scripture, confiding in our own understanding." Why? "Because the Spirit, who spoke by the prophets, is the only true interpreter of himself."[85]

Because of these references and others, Forstman noted: "In reading Calvin one may soon come to think that his favorite descriptive word for the Spirit is 'Teacher.'"[86] Ford Lewis Battles made a similar observation from his study of the *Institutes*. Calvin called "the Holy Spirit 'the inner teacher' (1.9.1; 3.1.4; 3.2.34; 4.14.9) or 'the schoolmaster' (4.17.36)"; and he called "Scripture the 'School of the Holy Spirit' (3.21.3)."[87] Those who submitted themselves to the Holy Spirit were "taught by means of the

---

81. Runia, "Hermeneutics of the Reformers," 145.

82. Rogers and McKim, *Authority and Interpretation of the Bible*, 104.

83. Forstman, *Word and Spirit*, 75–76. Also, see Calvin, *Commentaries on the Epistles of Paul the Apostle to the Philippians, Colossians, and Thessalonians*, 298, where Calvin said, "it is the proper office of the Spirit to illuminate the understandings of men."

84. Calvin, *Commentaries on the Catholic Epistles*, 389.

85. Calvin, *Commentary on the Epistles of Paul the Apostle to the Corinthians*, 117.

86. Forstman, *Word and Spirit*, 75.

87. Battles, "God Was Accommodating Himself to Human Capacity," 29–30.

word of God." Those who received and understood Scripture had been "inwardly taught by the Spirit," Calvin said.[88]

Fourth, Calvin's doctrine of the Spirit's close relationship to Scripture meant revelation was not given apart from Scripture. Calvin criticized the Enthusiasts for separating Word from Spirit. They claimed to receive revelation from God independently of the Word. Calvin declared: "The office of the Spirit . . . is not to feign new and unheard of revelations, . . . but to seal to our minds the same doctrine which the gospel delivers." According to Calvin, the Holy Spirit's role was not to impart new revelation, but rather to give confirmation and understanding of that revelation which had already been dispensed to the prophets and apostles.[89] The *testimonium* was not, then, the impartation of cognitive content in addition to the Word, but the illumination of Scripture's content which could not be fully comprehended apart from the Spirit's assistance.[90]

Finally, for Calvin, the Holy Spirit working by and through Scripture was God accommodating himself to human capacity. "Accommodation" was "the process of fitting, adapting, and adjusting language to the capacity of the hearers." That is, "the divinely appointed human authors of the Bible expressed the divine message under the Spirit's guidance in human forms of thought and speech so that all could benefit."[91] Thus, Calvin held a doctrine of the perspicuity of Scripture similar to that of Luther's; but Calvin did not hold so firmly to the right of individual private interpretation as did Luther. In Calvin's opinion, interpretation was not left entirely, or even primarily, to the individual.[92] In his commentary on Acts, he wrote: "We must remember, that the Scripture is not only given to us, but that interpreters and teachers are also added, to help us." In his *Institutes* he even recommended a "synod" or "council" of "true bishops" who could render consensus understandings.[93] Laity and

---

88. Calvin, *Institutes*, 2:429; and Calvin, *Institutes*, 1:90. Also, see Calvin, *Commentary on the Book of Psalms*, 5.

89. Calvin, *Institutes*, 1:106, 108.

90. Shelton, "Martin Luther's Concept of Biblical Interpretation," 298–307.

91. Rogers and McKim, *Authority and Interpretation of the Bible*, 98–99. See Battles, "Accommodating," for a complete discussion of Calvin's position.

92. Forstman, *Word and Spirit*, 78.

93. Calvin, *Commentary on the Acts of the Apostles*, 1:355; and Calvin, *Institutes*, 2:445.

clergy together, "having the Spirit for their leader and guide," could thus be assured of coming to correct interpretation of Scripture.[94]

Also, accommodation and illumination did not mean that normal study on the part of the interpreter was unnecessary. On the contrary, "Having an internal confidence in the Bible's authority, because of the testimony of the Holy Spirit, [Calvin] did not hesitate to seek understanding of the text through study."[95] He urged: "We must use all helps, which the Lord offereth unto us, for the understanding of the Scripture."[96] He sought to discover the obvious meaning by determining the original intention of the author. He recognized the importance of investigating the historical, geographical and cultural context of the passage.[97] Therefore, as in the case of Luther, Calvin's emphasis upon the role of the Holy Spirit was balanced by his appreciation of scholarship and his practice of responsible exegesis.

Reformed Scholasticism

Interpreters in the Post-Reformation era did not follow the earlier Reformers in all points. The steady rise of rationalism in the secular world on the one hand and the continuing extreme subjectivism of Enthusiasts on the other hand put constant pressure on Protestant orthodoxy. Gradually some adopted a rational approach to the Bible like that of Aquinas. They developed "a doctrine of Scripture that made the Bible a formal principle rather than a living witness." Following Aquinas, and contrary to Luther and Calvin, they put reason before faith and subjected the interpretation of the Bible itself to the light of human reason. This scholastic approach in the reformed tradition came to full development and was best exemplified in Francis Turretin (1623–1687). He came to occupy the chair of theology in Geneva about one century after Calvin's death.[98]

Much of Turretin's approach to Scripture and its interpretation was like that of the earlier Reformers. He emphasized the authority of

---

94. Calvin, *Commentary on the Acts of the Apostles*, 2:142.

95. Rogers and McKim, *Authority and Interpretation of the Bible*, 114.

96. Calvin, *Acts*, 1:355.

97. Kraus, "Calvin's Exegetical Principles," 12–16.

98. See Grant and Tracy, *Short History of the Interpretation of the Bible*, 100–1; and Rogers and McKim, *Authority and Interpretation of the Bible*, 172. Turretin is studied here also because of his special influence later on Princeton biblical interpretation.

Scripture, like Luther and Calvin, and developed a rather detailed and elaborate doctrine of inspiration.[99] Turretin affirmed the perspicuity of Scripture but admitted: "Scripture is obscure to unbelievers and . . . the illumination of the Spirit is needed by believers for its understanding." Perspicuity and illumination did not eliminate the need for the normal and necessary means of interpretation. Like the previous Reformers, he interpreted grammatically and historically. He denied the fourfold meaning concept developed during the Middle Ages and adopted by the Roman Catholics of his day.[100]

Regardless of his similarities to the earlier Reformers, Turretin's basic approach to Scripture was opposite to theirs with regard to the relationship of faith and reason. Like Aquinas, Turretin placed reason before faith in that he "concluded that mankind could reason from the natural light to some knowledge of God." He developed a rational approach to Scripture, even resorting to "rational proofs to prove the Bible's inspiration and inerrancy" in order to assure Scripture's authority. Allison noted that this was "a radical departure from the concept of Calvin."[101]

As stated above, Turretin did say that the illumination of the Holy Spirit was necessary for understanding. Allison, however, concluded: "[Turretin] was afraid of any type of subjective experience with the Spirit. The fanaticism of the Anabaptists was repulsive to him." He thus attacked the Anabaptists for relying upon immediate revelations from the Holy Spirit.[102] According to Rogers and McKim, Turretin therein began a move that narrowly confined the work of the Holy Spirit in relationship to Scripture. Thereafter, especially in the Princeton theologians, "a successive narrowing of the role of the Holy Spirit was evidenced as Reformed scholasticism continued to develop."[103]

---

99. See chapter 4, "The Authority of Scripture," in Turretin, *The Doctrine of Scripture*, 39–55; and Allison, "The Doctrine of Scripture in the Theology of John Calvin and Francis Turretin," 59–61.

100. Turretin, *The Doctrine of Scripture*, 185–87, 199–208.

101. Allison, "The Doctrine of Scripture in the Theology of John Calvin and Francis Turretin," 59–61.

102. Ibid., 65.

103. Rogers and McKim, *Authority and Interpretation of the Bible*, 174–76.

English Reformation

While Turretin was leading the way of scholasticism, the English Reformation was undergoing a separate development distinct from what was evolving on the continent. In 1643, a decade before Turretin was named professor of theology in Geneva, the Westminster Assembly of Divines began meeting in Westminster Abbey. Three years later they completed the famous Westminster Confession of Faith. The smaller committee responsible for drafting the document was comprised of seven Englishmen (Cornelius Burges, Thomas Gataker, Robert Harris, Charles Herle, Joshua Hoyle, Edward Reynolds, and Thomas Temple) and four Scots (Robert Baillie, George Gillespie, Alexander Henderson, and Samuel Rutherford).[104]

The first chapter of the Westminster Confession of Faith was entitled, "Of the Holy Scripture." It sat forth a doctrine of Scripture and approach to hermeneutics that was much like that of the earlier Continental Reformers. The first section affirmed "the Holy Scripture" as special revelation that was "necessary unto salvation." After listing both the Old and New Testament books common to Protestant Bibles, the second section declared that all of these books were "given by inspiration of God to be the rule of faith and life." (The third section of the chapter specifically denied divine inspiration for the "books commonly called Apocrypha.") Section four asserted "the authority of the Holy Scripture." This authority did not depend upon "the testimony of any man, or church; but wholly upon God . . . the author thereof." It was to be believed, obeyed, and received because it was "the Word of God." This was followed in the fifth section by a statement that echoed Calvin's *testimonium*. "Our full persuasion and assurance of the infallible truth and divine authority thereof, is from the inward work of the Holy Spirit."[105]

The last five sections in the first chapter of the Westminster Confession dealt with how to interpret Scripture. Concerning the perspicuity of Scripture, the Westminster Divines acknowledged varying levels of clarity. Therefore, study with "due use of ordinary means" was appropriate and necessary. However, "those things which are necessary to be known, believed, and observed for salvation, are so clearly pro-

---

104. Ibid., 200–1.

105. These citations of the Westminster Confession of Faith are from "Appendix: Reformed Confessions on Scripture" (462–71) in Rogers and McKim, *Authority and Interpretation of the Bible*, 468–70.

pounded, . . . that not only the learned, but the unlearned . . . may attain unto a sufficient understanding of them." Also, the Holy Spirit was seen to play a vital role in understanding Scripture adequately. The Divines said: "We acknowledge the inward illumination of the Spirit of God to be necessary for the saving understanding of such things as are revealed in the Word." Finally, "the supreme judge" who determined the correctness of all understandings was "no other but the Holy Spirit speaking in the Scripture."[106]

Two points should be especially noted here. One, the Westminster Divines followed Augustine and the early Reformers (not Aquinas and Turretin) by giving priority to faith. "Faith not only took precedence over reason, but for the Divines, faith was the only way to know spiritual matters." Two, the Westminster Divines—by properly acknowledging both the need for scholarly study and the role of the Holy Spirit—did not fail to balance the objective and subjective sides of biblical herme-neutics. Thus, "despite sectarian appeals to the Spirit, the Divines did not overreact as did the later Protestant scholastics who banished all illumination of the Spirit from the interpretation of Scripture."[107]

The impact of the Westminster Confession is well attested. Several of its authors—especially Reynolds, Baillie, Gillespie, and Rutherford—affirmed and reaffirmed its positions in their own writings.[108] A decade later John Owen (1616–1683) participated in drawing up the Savoy Declaration that essentially reproduced the Westminster Confession.[109] Later, Owen greatly extended the influence of these confessions by his extensive writings.

Included among Owen's works was a large *Discourse on the Holy Spirit*. Book VI, Part II, "Causes, Ways, and Means of Understanding the Mind of God," amounted to a hermeneutics primer based upon the Westminster Confession. There Owen told how to come to a correct understanding of Scripture. He discussed the importance of the "ecclesiastical" means (views of other "holy and learned" persons and groups)

---

106. Ibid.

107. Ibid., 203, 209.

108. For a more complete study of these, see Rogers, *Scripture in the Westminster Confession: A Problem of Historical Interpretation for American Presbyterianism.*

109. Rogers and McKim, *Authority and Interpretation of the Bible*, 218–19.

and the necessity of the "disciplinary" means (scholarly studies); but his highest priority was the "Spiritual" means.[110]

Apparently, Owen's primary purpose in this emphasis was twofold. One, it was to affirm the privilege of individual interpretation against the Roman doctrine of exclusive ecclesiastical infallibility. Two, his purpose was to show the correct nature of the Spirit's illumination against the Enthusiasts' claims of new immediate external revelation from the Holy Spirit. He planned to show that "there is no safety in depending on *enthusiasms*, or immediate pretended infallible inspirations, nor on the *pretended infallibility* of any church." He explained: "There is an *internal subjective revelation*, whereby no *new things* are revealed unto our minds, . . . but our minds are enabled to discern things that are revealed already."[111]

With this intermediate position in view, Owen repeatedly contended that illumination by the Holy Spirit was absolutely necessary to a full understanding of Scripture. He wrote:

> In the *mere exercise of our own natural reason and understanding* . . . we cannot attain that knowledge of the mind and will of God in the Scripture . . . without the special aid and assistance of the Holy Spirit of God. Wherefore, principally, it is asserted, . . . there is an especial work of the Holy Spirit, in the *supernatural illumination* of our minds . . . that we may aright . . . understand the mind of God in the Scripture ourselves, or interpret it unto others.[112]

He continued for a total of fifty pages to discuss the Spiritual illumination of Scripture. He remained rather general in his explanation of exactly how the Holy Spirit works and specifically what he reveals in illumination. Nevertheless, Owen's work was a major contribution in that it brought together, with some development and refinement, ideas that had been held from Origen through Augustine and the early Reformers.

---

110. Owen, *Works*, 4:117–234.

111. Ibid., 4:127.

112. Ibid., 4:125–26. Owen's discourse is one of the longest early discussions of the role of the Holy Spirit in hermeneutics.

Summary

During the Reformation and Post-Reformation era those leading the way in understanding Scripture regarded the Bible as the highest authority in all theological discussions. Correct interpretation was of utmost importance. They emphasized and insisted on interpretation that was based upon a proper historical and grammatical understanding of the Bible. "But their exegesis was never merely historical. It began in the letter but it necessarily proceeded under the guidance of the Spirit." Usually, faith was placed before reason. Turretin, however, developed a scholasticism in which the Spirit's role was de-emphasized and Scripture no longer spoke so much to the heart as to "the critical intellect."[113] Notwithstanding, in the English Reformation, the Westminster Divines and Owen reemphasized the role of the Holy Spirit in interpretation.

ENLIGHTENMENT TO MID-TWENTIETH CENTURY

In 1678, five years before the death of Owen, the French priest Richard Simon began publishing a series of books in which he applied critical methods to the Bible. Edgar Krentz credited Simon with thereby becoming "the direct founder of the historical-critical study of the Bible." By the end of that century a new age had dawned. "A new world view and a new inductive science that concerned itself with this world, not with Aristotle's unseen teleological mover, were born." Whereas "at the beginning of the seventeenth century the Bible was the universal authority in all fields of knowledge, . . . by the end of the century that authority had eroded."[114] The seventeenth century thus ushered in the "Age of Reason," and the eighteenth century, with its revolutionary new insights in all fields (including biblical studies), became known as the "Age of Enlightenment."[115]

In biblical studies, responses to the Enlightenment's advances varied from enthusiastic acceptance to reactionary opposition. The growing influence of rationalism and free thought opened the doors to radically new proposals in hermeneutics and also spawned counter reactions against perceived threats to traditional approaches. The more significant of these responses and reactions were included in the developments of

---

113. Grant and Tracy, *Short History of the Interpretation of the Bible*, 93, 97.

114. Krentz, *Historical-Critical Method*, 11, 15.

115. Brown, "The Enlightenment," 355

historical-critical studies, American Reformed scholasticism, Roman Catholic modernism, and Neo-orthodoxy.

Historical-Critical Studies

The Enlightenment's primary bequest to Christendom was scientific or critical interpretation of the Bible. The method came to be called the "historical-critical method."[116] During the Ecumenical Study Conference at Wadham College in Oxford in 1949 the method was described by stating the steps in its procedure. These included: (1) determination of the text; (2) analysis of the literary form of the passage; (3) investigation of the historical situation, the *Sitz im Leben*; (4) determination of the meaning which the words had for the author and the original hearers or readers; and (5) understanding of the passage in the light of its total context and the background out of which it emerged.[117]

While Simon, as stated above, may be called the "direct founder of the historical-critical study of the Bible," the basic elements of critical study did not originate with him. Also, he did not develop what is now known as the "historical-critical method." As Krentz pointed out, the roots of criticism extended back at least into the Renaissance and Reformation. Humanists like Erasmus and Colet and the Reformers including Luther, Calvin, and Zwingli all raised critical questions and issues in their study of Scripture. Following the publication of Simon's series, men like Locke, Hume, and Lessing made their contributions that not only prepared the way for, but also called for a new approach to the Bible. Gradually, theologians began to arrive at a more historical and critical interpretation of the Bible.[118] During the first half of the nineteenth century "the critical historical method . . . came to be regarded as the only legitimate kind of exegesis."[119]

The theologian who dominated the nineteenth century and most promoted this method was Friedrich Schleiermacher (1768–1834). He "exercised a profound influence alike on religion and on biblical interpretation."[120] "Schleiermacher's enthusiastic and unqualified accep-

116. For a thorough summary of the history and nature of the historical-critical method, the reader should see Krentz, *Historical-Critical Method*, cited above.

117. Krentz, *Historical-Critical Method*, 2.

118. Ibid., 7–18.

119. Grant and Tracy, *Short History of the Interpretation of the Bible*, 110.

120. Farrar, *History of Interpretation*, 409.

tance of the principle of historical criticism mark[ed] a turning point of crucial importance." His approach to Scripture and theology became "the framework, as it were, of the characteristic theological outlook of the century."[121]

This theological outlook was "generally styled Liberal Protestant-ism."[122] It grew up apart from church control because with Schleier-macher the scene of biblical studies "shifted to the secularized German universities, where distinct philosophical presuppositions guided the historical investigations." The rationalists' attitude toward miracles and view of the universe controlled by fixed laws that allowed for no suspen-sion or alteration were taken for granted.[123]

One of Schleiermacher's most significant principles was that the Bible was not fundamentally different from other ancient literature, and it was to be interpreted as any other book. He considered the issue of "whether on account of the Holy Spirit the Scriptures must be treated in a special way." Schleiermacher concluded: "The Holy Spirit could have spoken through them [the authors] only as they themselves would have spoken." Thus, although he used the term "inspiration," the old theories of inspiration were meaningless to Schleiermacher and those who fol-lowed him.[124] He contended:

> Inspiration . . . should not influence the work of interpretation. If in the case of the Bible, as in every other case, the goal of herme-neutics is to understand the texts as their original readers un-derstood them, the fact that they are inspired does not affect the

---

121. Richardson, *The Bible in the Age of Science*, 78, 79.

122. Ibid., 84. Neill noted: "The name of Schleiermacher became a kind of bogey word, as standing for infidelity." Neill, *The Interpretation of the New Testament: 1861–1961*, 9.

123. Mickelsen, *Interpreting the Bible*, 44. This was the view of most of the early devel-opers of the historical-critical method. Consequently, orthodox and conservative scholars rejected the method at first. However, as Krentz notes, this is not the case today. Most scholars now realize that these earlier presuppositions are not inherent in the method. "It is a truism today to assert that historical research is no longer historicistic and positivistic. There is a changed climate in science and history that no longer is as certain of the uni-versality and immutability of laws." Krentz believes "the integration of faith and historical method has been accomplished" in recent years. There is a general consensus about the acceptance of the method. Krentz, *Historical-Critical Method*, 2–5, 59, 68–69.

124. Grant and Tracy, *Short History of the Interpretation of the Bible*, 113. Neill, stated: "Schleiermacher's view . . . was incompatible with a belief in verbal inspiration." Neill, *Interpretation of the New Testament*, 9.

interpretation at all. Therefore, there is no special hermeneutics for the New Testament because it is inspired.[125]

Thus, in response to the question, "are the books of Holy Scripture as such in a different category than secular books," Schleiermacher answered, "no."[126]

Since the Bible was "a purely human product without any genuine interventions (acts) of God as its base or guidance of God in its production," Schleiermacher simply approached the interpretation of Scripture as he would any other material.[127] He stated: "Neither its language nor its genre requires that there be a special hermeneutics for the Bible, nor does its double layers of meaning."[128] Thus, Grant noted that "the idea of interpreting the Bible in the same way as any other book was popularized by Schleiermacher."[129]

Also, for Schleiermacher there was no such thing as a role of the Holy Spirit in interpretation. He disdained the idea of illumination. He held that such an idea led to "a dogmatic system of concepts" and resulted in confusion and "unscientific excess." Rather, the Bible could be interpreted as any other book by relying solely on the tools used to interpret other similar ancient writings.[130]

Following Schleiermacher, Ernst Troeltsch (1865–1923), and Rudolf Bultmann (1884–1976) further developed the principles and practices of the historical-critical method. In his essay, "On Historical and Dogmatic Method in Theology" (1898), Troeltsch formulated his principles of historical criticism: (1) the principle of criticism; (2) the principle of analogy; and (3) the principle of correlation.[131] The third one of these implies that all historical phenomena are interrelated in an unbroken chain of cause and effect. Bultmann also became well known for viewing history

---

125. Schleiermacher, *Hermeneutics*, 107, 216.

126. Ibid., 67.

127. Mickelsen, *Interpreting the Bible*, 44–45.

128. Schleiermacher, *Hermeneutics*, 215.

129. Grant and Tracy, *Short History of the Interpretation of the Bible*, 111.

130. Schleiermacher, 103, 106, 145. Grant pointed out, however, that even in the mid-nineteenth century in the universities where objective research was maintained, not all critics followed the radical school. For example, Beck (1804–1878), a noted scholar at Tubingen, "upheld the inspiration of the writers of scripture and the possibility of spiritual (pneumatic) exegesis." Grant and Tracy, *Short History of the Interpretation of the Bible*, 112.

131. Morgan, *Introduction to Ernst Troeltsch*, 10.

as a closed continuum of cause and effect—a view of history that allowed only causation that was not theological nor transcendental.[132]

To say that nineteenth-century style historical criticism changed the way that the Bible was viewed and studied would be an understatement. The change was so profound that scholars generally agree with Kurt Mueller-Vollmer who said: "With Schleiermacher, modern hermeneutics begins."[133] Troeltsch's first and second principles supported Schleiermacher's position that the Bible should not be treated in any special way but rather interpreted like any other book. Troeltsch's second and third principles led to Bultmann's conclusion that miracles and salvation history must be ruled out *a priori*.[134] The reader should especially note the significance of Troeltsch's position relative to the idea of a role of the Holy Spirit in hermeneutics. Such a notion could find no compatible ground with the historical-critical method when Troeltsch's principles were strictly maintained and when his method was the final word in understanding the Bible.

Naturally, these new views and approaches to the study of Scripture met with strong resistance in orthodox Protestant circles. Acceptance of the historical-critical method came only after the passing of time and then only with certain qualifications and modifications. By the middle of the twentieth century most biblical scholars had reached two primary conclusions regarding the method. One, Troeltsch's type was untenable. Two, historical criticism was both valuable and necessary when properly understood and applied.[135] Obviously, the principle of correlation, as maintained by Troeltsch, was unable to acknowledge a transcendent God's acts in history. It had a blind spot for divine causation. Evangelical scholars concluded that the Bible was not an ordinary book and Troeltsch's type of historical-critical method could not do justice to the essence of the biblical message. His principles were not to be totally discarded, however. They were to be modified or qualified. For example, the principle of correlation was seen to be valid as long as it was made open to all possible causes in history—including God's activity.[136]

---

132. Krentz, *Historical-Critical Method*, 58.

133. Mueller-Vollmer, *Preface to The Hermeneutics Reader*, xi.

134. See Greidanus, *The Modern Preacher and the Ancient Text*, 55–58.

135. The reader should see Krentz's discussion of this in *Historical-Critical Method*, 73–88.

136. See Greidanus, *Modern Preacher and the Ancient Text*, 33, 35, 36–37.

Presently, scholars generally agree with Krentz: "Theology cannot return to a precritical age. . . . The Bible is an ancient book addressed to people of long ago in a strange culture, written in ancient languages. Historical criticism respects this historical gap."[137] Peter Stuhlmacher believes that scholars now have the possibility of "making use of historical criticism where it is really productive, namely in historical analysis and description, and at the same time of transcending it where it threatens to restrict . . . encounter with historical reality."[138] The historical-critical method is valuable even though there is a transcendent or divine dimension in biblical history with which it is unable to deal.[139] Thus, contemporary scholars conclude that, along with historical criticism, the role of the Holy Spirit in hermeneutics must be taken seriously.[140]

Roman Catholic Modernism

Roman Catholic interpretation of Scripture was also unable to escape being affected by the "heavy seas of biblical criticism." The political leaders of the church were able to prevent a major move by indexing offensive writings and excommunicating "heretics." The list of "liberal" writings placed on the Index steadily lengthened throughout the nineteenth century.[141] Nevertheless, the scholars who produced these writings succeeded in developing what became known as "Modernism."[142]

H. F. R. de Lamennais (1782–1854), a French priest, was a forerunner of this movement. He contended that Catholicism was not confirmed chiefly by miracles and fulfilled prophecies, but by its capacity to perpetuate those beliefs which mankind had found essential to an ordered social life. Later, leading "modernists" followed Lamennais' new apologetic for Catholicism with an anthropocentric and antidogmatic

---

137. Krentz, *Historical-Critical Method*, 61.

138. Stuhlmacher, *Historical Criticism and Theological Interpretation of Scripture*, 90.

139. See Hasel, *Old Testament Theology*, 171–73.

140. See Krentz, *Historical Critical Method*, 70. Significantly, Neill, in *Interpretation of the New Testament*, 235, suggests that Bultmann's major problem was his "lack of a theology of the Holy Spirit, as the one through whom time and distance are annihilated, and through whom the Word of Jesus becomes the living and contemporary word."

141. Grant and Tracy, *Short History of the Interpretation of the Bible*, 119.

142. Vidler, *The Modernist Movement in the Roman Church*, xi–xii.

approach to theology. These modernists included: Alfred Loisy, George Tyrrell, Edouard Le Roy, Mauride Blondel, and Ernesto Buonaiuti.[143]

Grant suggested that the "culmination of modernist interpretation" was found in *The Gospel and the Church*, by Alfred Loisy (1857–1940), first published in French in 1902 and later translated into English. Loisy intended this to be a Catholic response to Harnack's unorthodox views. Instead of being well received, however, it eventually resulted in Loisy's excommunication. This was because in this work he not only criticized Harnack but also the official Roman Catholic theory of the interpretation of Scripture.[144] Apparently accepting the current historical-critical approach, Loisy wrote: "The work of traditional exegesis . . . seems in permanent contradiction with the principles of a purely rational and historical interpretation."[145]

Like Schleiermacher, Loisy rejected the traditional view of the Bible beginning with the doctrine of inspiration. He wrote:

> He compromises God who makes him the author of written books. . . . Theologians tax their wits to explain how God can be, in any real sense, the author of books which he has neither written himself nor dictated word by word. . . . What anthropomorphism could be more naive than that which counts the authorship of books among the attributes of God?[146]

With regret Loisy noted: "To this notion of divine authorship, so artificial and fragile, the church committed her future and compromised it in so doing." He added: "The books reputed all divine are simply not filled with truth from beginning to end—far from it! They contain as many errors as books of their kind, written when they were, could be made to hold." He concluded: "Not only at this starting point [divine authorship], but along the whole line of historical and literary criticism, the traditional doctrine is in complete collapse."[147]

Loisy went on to reject almost the entire traditional doctrine of the supernatural character and content of the Bible. He described the supernaturalism of the Bible as "a mixture of magic and mythology" that was simply "unthinkable by contemporary intelligence." He did not totally

---

143. Piggin, "Liberal Catholicism," 200.

144. Grant and Tracy, *Short History of the Interpretation of the Bible*, 121.

145. Loisy, *The Gospel and the Church*, 219.

146. Loisy, *The Origins of the New Testament*, 10, 15.

147. Ibid., 11–12.

discount the idea of the supernatural, "but to look for a clear conception or express formulation of it [even] in the New Testament would be the most childish of anachronisms. We find it there only in germ, embedded in supernatural magic."[148]

Although Loisy never commented directly about the Holy Spirit's involvement in the interpretation of Scripture, it seems apparent that he would have rejected such a notion. As noted above, he criticized the traditional Catholic theory of the interpretation that from the times of Origen and Augustine had included the idea of the Holy Spirit's role in the endeavor. Also, as just stated, he greatly discounted the notion of the supernatural associated with the Bible. Therefore, like Schleiermacher and others in Protestant liberalism, Loisy presumably would have rejected the notion of a role of the Holy Spirit in hermeneutics.

American Reformed Scholasticism

While many in the scholarly world flowed with the currents of the Enlightenment, others resisted its floods. Besides the resistance of the Roman Catholic hierarchy noted above, one of the most significant reactionary responses to the revolutionary new insights of the Enlightenment was that advanced in American Reformed scholasticism. This developed primarily from Princeton Theological Seminary. Archibald Alexander (1772–1851) led the Presbyterian Church in establishing Princeton Theological Seminary in 1812. He "constructed the framework which shaped the theology at the seminary for over a century." The leading theologians at Princeton after Alexander were Charles Hodge (1797–1878), A. A. Hodge (1823–1886), and B. B. Warfield (1851–1921). These men were responsible for firming up the seminary's view of and approach to the Bible.[149]

Alexander and the Princeton theologians following him attempted to take a stand regarding revelation between two opposing positions—that of the Deists on the one hand and that of the Enthusiasts on the other hand. Following the scientific revolution of the sixteenth and seventeenth centuries, regard for the idea of natural revelation progressively changed. At first, it was seen as useful support for special revelation. Next, natural revelation was regarded as equal to special revelation.

148. Ibid., 21, 27, 31.
149. Noll, *Introduction to The Princeton Theology, 1812-1921,* 13–16.

Later, it was held to be superior to special revelation. Finally, deists declared natural revelation to be the only revelation. At the other extreme, the enthusiasts claimed to receive a special revelation of "inner light" imparted directly by the Holy Spirit apart from Scripture. They held this revelation to be equal to or superior to the revelation of Scripture. Alexander and the other Princeton theologians sought to demonstrate the insufficiency of natural revelation on the one hand and the absolute completeness of biblical revelation on the other hand.[150]

In his attempt to establish and maintain a position between that of the Deists and the Enthusiasts, Alexander affirmed a strong dogma of biblical authority based on the doctrine of verbal inspiration. He also held to and practiced traditional approaches to interpretation of Scripture. Further, he centered the seminary studies in the works of Turretin. In this move, Alexander unwittingly led the Princetonians into following Turretin in placing reason prior to faith.[151]

Since, as noted above, Turretin had developed a scholastic approach to Scripture, Alexander thus started down the road of scholasticism. He further moved in that direction by accepting and using Scottish Common Sense Philosophy. Noll explained:

> Scottish Common Sense Realism was a philosophy designed expressly to save the benefits of England's "moderate" Scientific Revolution for good theology. It was a pointed view . . . which attempted to refute the skepticism of David Hume. This approach . . . argued that normal people, using responsibly the information provided by their senses, actually grasped thereby the real world.[152]

Noll added, "this Scottish thought was the chrysalis from which the Princeton Theology emerged. It was brought to America from Scotland . . . by the Rev. John Witherspoon, who . . . taught the teachers of Princeton Theology."[153] Rogers and McKim observed:

> The rudiments of the Princeton theology as set forth by Archibald Alexander remained unchanged for over one hundred years. But the emphases did change as the Princeton theologians rigidified in the face of mounting opposition to their scholastic style.[154]

150. Sandeen, "The Princeton Theology," 309.

151. Rogers and McKim, *Authority and Interpretation of the Bible*, 268–69.

152. Noll, *Introduction to Princeton Theology*, 13, 30–31.

153. Ibid., 31.

154. Rogers and McKim, *Authority and Interpretation of the Bible*, 273.

Of special interest was the fact that "a successive narrowing of the role of the Holy Spirit was evidenced as Reformed scholasticism continued to develop."[155] This was especially the case with regard to the interpretation of Scripture. In his inaugural address at Princeton in 1812, Alexander addressed this topic. He began: "How should the Scriptures be interpreted in order that we may arrive at their *true* and *full* meaning? The obvious answer would be, by attending to the grammatical and literal sense of the words employed." After further elaboration, he concluded his address with these thoughts about the role of the Holy Spirit. "A help which, though put in the last place in this discourse, is of more real importance than all the rest; is *the illumination and assistance of the Holy Spirit.*" He said he was "convinced that without the divine assistance" the interpreter had "little hope of arriving at the knowledge of the truth."[156]

Alexander's same firm certainty of the Spirit's role was not maintained throughout by following scholastic-minded Princetonians. Charles Hodge began his great *Systematic Theology* with a discussion of the right use of reason and a comparison of theology with the study of natural science. He wrote:

> The Bible is to the theologian what nature is to the man of science. It is his store-house of facts; and his method of ascertaining what the Bible teaches is the same as that which the natural philosopher adopts to ascertain what nature teaches.[157]

He viewed the theologian's work with the data of Scripture to be analogous to the scientist's work with the data of nature. Sandeen noted that Hodge consistently insisted "the witness of the Spirit, the mystical strain, be subordinated to the matter of theological science" which was found in the Bible. "This attempt to adapt theology to the methodology of Newtonian science produced a wooden, mechanical discipline as well as a rigorously logical one."[158]

The rigorously scholastic approach to Scripture along with a successive narrowing of the role of the Holy Spirit continued with both A. A. Hodge and B. B. Warfield. By the time Warfield became the leading Princeton theologian his approach allowed "the work of the Holy Spirit

155. Ibid., 175.
156. Alexander, "Inaugural Address," 81–85.
157. Hodge, *Systematic Theology*, 1:10.
158. Sandeen, "The Princeton Theology," 310.

only in inspiring the original authors of Scripture, and not at all in enabling modern readers to understand their Bibles."[159]

Warfield placed the locus of the Spirit's most significant work at the past point of inspiration. In an essay written in 1915 he declared:

> The value of "inspiration" emerges, thus, as twofold. It gives to the books written under its "bearing" a quality which is truly superhuman; a trustworthiness, an authority, a searchingness, a profundity, a profitableness which is altogether Divine. And [inspiration] speaks this Divine word immediately to each reader's heart.[160]

Because of his concept of the already accomplished results of "inspiration," Warfield discredited the notion that "[God] cannot be known save by a supernatural action of the Holy Spirit." He stated: "The knowledge of God to which a man attains through the testimony of the Spirit is therefore the knowledge which belongs to him as normal man."[161]

Warfield further revealed his view of the Holy Spirit's role in hermeneutics in an essay on Calvin's doctrine of the *testimonium Spiritus Sancti*. He said he wrote the essay "to guard against misapprehension of [Calvin's doctrine]." He understood Calvin's doctrine to mean that "the testimony of the Spirit concerns the accrediting of Scripture, not the assimilation of its revelatory contents." Warfield explained: "The whole function of the Spirit with respect to the truth is, *not to reveal to us the truth anew*, [my emphasis] much less to reveal to us new truth, but efficaciously to confirm the Word, revealed in the Scriptures." He believed that "to attribute to [the Holy Spirit] repeated or new revelations to each of the children of God . . . is derogatory to the Word, which is his inspired product."[162] For Warfield there was no present role for the Holy Spirit to play in the understanding of God's inspired Word.

American Reformed Scholasticism was a reactionary response to the skeptical attitudes of the eighteenth century Enlightenment. In most ways, its views of and approaches to the Bible were directly opposite to those of so-called "liberalism." Its Princeton Seminary leaders affirmed a strong position on biblical authority based upon the doctrine of verbal inspiration of an inerrant text. They practiced traditional approaches

---

159. Rogers and McKim, *Authority and Interpretation of the Bible*, 176.

160. Warfield, "Inspiration," 288.

161. Warfield, *Calvin and Augustine*, 151.

162. Warfield, *Calvin and Augustine*, 71, 79, 81–82.

to interpreting Scripture. In resistance to Schleiermacher and others, Charles Hodge "determinedly opposed all attempts to subject the Bible to the same analysis as other books."[163] The early Princetonians also posited a role of the Spirit in the hermeneutical process. Ironically, however, like "liberalism," American Reformed scholasticism's ultimate hermeneutic, which was developed by its later leaders, excluded the Holy Spirit from a role in interpretation.

Neo-orthodoxy

At the same time that Warfield's scholastic approach was limiting the Holy Spirit's role, Karl Barth (1886–1968), in Germany, was leading the way with a different kind of response to the Enlightenment milieu. Neo-orthodoxy, as this new movement came to be called, was at the same time "a rejection of Protestant scholasticism, and . . . a denial of the Protestant liberal movement."[164] Its view of Scripture and approach to Scripture were in opposition to both liberalism and scholasticism. Contrary to liberalism, Neo-orthodoxy held Holy Scripture was to be heard as the authoritative Word of God. Contrary to scholasticism, Neo-orthodoxy held Holy Scripture was not to be exactly equated, without qualification, to the fullest form of the Word of God, which was Jesus Christ.[165]

"The first important expression of [Neo-orthodoxy] was Karl Barth's *Romerbrief*, published in 1919."[166] Other scholars soon joined the movement, but Barth's initial impact and continuing influence were so profound that Neo-orthodoxy became a new theological era associated with his name.[167] Many observers have agreed with Grant's evaluation: "No one did more [than Barth] to recover the authority of the Bible for our day."[168]

For Barth, and those who followed him, the Bible was like no other book. He stated: "Scripture is holy and the Word of God, because by the Holy Spirit it became and will become to the church a witness to divine revelation."[169] In Barth's view, Scripture was one form of the three-

---

163. Rogers and McKim, *Authority and Interpretation of the Bible*, 279.

164. Schnucker, "Neo-Orthodoxy," 754.

165. See Mueller, *Karl Barth*, 55–58.

166. Schnucker, "Neo-Orthodoxy," 754.

167. Mueller, *Karl Barth*, 23.

168. Grant and Tracy, *Short History of the Interpretation of the Bible*, 133.

169. Barth, *The Doctrine of the Word of God*, 457.

fold "Word of God": (1) the Word proclaimed, preaching; (2) the Word written, Scripture; and (3) the Word revealed, Jesus Christ.[170] He wrote: "Scripture is recognized as the Word of God by the fact that it *is* the Word of God. This is what we are told by the doctrine of the witness of the Holy Spirit."[171]

Barth clarified his conception of the Bible as the Word of God. While Scripture was recognized as "the Word of God," he made it clear that the Bible itself was not its fullest form. Jesus Christ himself was the fullest form of the Word of God. "There is only one Word of God and that is the eternal Word of the Father which . . . became flesh like us and has now returned to the Father, to be presented to his church by the Holy Spirit."[172] However, Barth also noted: "The Bible is the concrete medium by which the church recalls God's revelation in the past, is called to expect revelation in the future, and is thereby challenged, empowered, and guided to proclaim."[173]

Barth's view of the Bible had definite implications for his interpretation of Scripture. One implication was simply that the Bible needed interpretation. "Human words need interpretation because they are ambiguous. . . . Now, since God's Word in Scripture has taken the form of a human word, it has itself incurred the need of such interpretation." He added that presently "to interpret God's Word must and can now mean to interpret Holy Scripture."[174]

Two, in Barth's consideration of Scripture, historical criticism was "only a preliminary step in the task of interpretation."[175] He asserted:

> The historical-critical method of Biblical investigation has its rightful place: it is concerned with the preparation of the intelligence—and this can never be superfluous. But, were I driven to choose between it and the venerable doctrine of Inspiration, I should without hesitation adopt the latter. . . . The doctrine of Inspiration is concerned with the labor of apprehending, without which no technical equipment, however complete, is of any use whatever.[176]

170. Barth, *Church Dogmatics*, 1.1.88–124.

171. Barth, *Church Dogmatics*, 1.2.537.

172. Barth, *Church Dogmatics*, 1.2.512–13.

173. Barth, *Church Dogmatics*, 1.1.124–25.

174. Barth, *Church Dogmatics*, 1.2.712–13.

175. Krentz, *Historical-Critical Method*, 30, 68.

176. Barth, *The Epistle to the Romans*, 1.

Barth held that "a reading of Scripture that did not pass beyond merely the understanding of its words, paragraphs, and histories was not enough."[177] His goal in interpretation was "to see through and beyond history into the spirit of the Bible, which is the Eternal Spirit."[178]

Third, Barth's position raised once again the question of the relationship of faith to the interpretative process. Barth's answer was that faith was a necessary prerequisite to understanding Scripture. Scripture had to be approached by faith in prayer. He held that when the Bible spoke to a person as the Word of God it was the result of an awakening and strengthening of that person's faith. Barth considered this witness of and from Scripture to be a "miracle." "We can and should therefore pray that this witness may be made to us. But it does not lie . . . in our power but only in God's, that this event should take place and therefore this witness of Scripture be made to us."[179]

Barth's view of the Bible had yet a fourth and most important implication for interpretation of Scripture—the Spirit's role was absolutely necessary. This implication was derived from Barth's view of the Holy Spirit's close relationship to Scripture. He saw "the Holy Spirit active both in the inspiration of the biblical writers and in making their witness a living Word of God through the ages."[180] In his *Church Dogmatics*, Barth began his section on "The Outpouring of the Holy Spirit" with the following statement. "According to Holy Scripture God's revelation occurs in our enlightenment by the Holy Spirit of God to a knowledge of his Word." Later in that discussion he wrote: "The reason, and the only reason, why man can receive revelation in the Holy Spirit is that God's Word is brought to his hearing in the Holy Spirit."[181]

Here one must keep in mind Barth's concept of "God's Word" and of "revelation." As noted above, Barth understood the "Word of God" to be threefold: proclamation; Scripture; and Jesus Christ. He understood "revelation" to consist of two aspects: the objective reality of revelation, Jesus Christ; and the subjective reality of revelation, the Holy Spirit. Also, again as noted above, according to Barth, "to interpret God's Word must and can *now* [my emphasis] mean to interpret Holy Scripture."

177. Rogers and McKim, *Authority and Interpretation of the Bible*, 415.

178. Barth, *Epistle to the Romans*, 1.

179. Barth, *Church Dogmatics*, 1.2.512, 531.

180. Mueller, *Karl Barth*, 57.

181. Barth, *Church Dogmatics*, 1.2.203, 247.

Further, the Word of God presently reaches humanity as "the subjective reality of revelation."[182]

Barth further explained the relationship of objective and subjective revelation and the role of the Holy Spirit in bringing it to man. He said, by the Holy Spirit, "the objective reality of revelation becomes a subjective reality."[183] Barth explained:

> Subjective revelation is not the addition of a second revelation to objective revelation. . . . Subjective revelation can consist only in the fact that objective revelation, the one truth which cannot be added to or bypassed, comes to man and is . . . acknowledged by man. And that is the work of the Holy Spirit.[184]

He added: "The work of the Holy Spirit is that our blind eyes are opened, . . . the Holy Spirit draws and takes us right into the reality of revelation by doing what we cannot do, by opening our eyes and ears and hearts." Barth concluded: "If the church lives by the Bible because it is the Word of God, that means that it lives by the fact that Christ is revealed in the Bible by the work of the Holy Spirit."[185] "The Holy Ghost knows very well what he has said to the prophets and apostles and what through them he wills also to say to us."[186] Thus, as David Mueller observed, Barth repeatedly emphasized the Holy Spirit as the "teacher of the Word."[187]

Finally, Mueller also noted Barth's hesitancy concerning any description of "how" God works through his Spirit.[188] Since it was a "miracle," Barth held that "how" the Spirit brought this revelation to man's understanding through Scripture was beyond one's ability to explain. "About that work there is nothing specific that we can say," Barth suggested. "We have to respect the mystery of the given-ness of this fact as such, i.e., as the inconceivable and therefore the unspeakable mystery of the person and work of God."[189]

---

182. Ibid., 1–25, 203–40, 204, 717.

183. Ibid., 233.

184. Ibid., 238–39.

185. Ibid., 239–40, 513.

186. Ibid., 712.

187. Mueller, *Karl Barth*, 82.

188. Ibid., 80.

189. Barth, *Church Dogmatics*, 1.2.233, 239.

Summary

During the eighteenth and nineteenth centuries the attitudes and insights of the Age of Enlightenment dramatically impacted biblical studies. The rise of rationalism and critical studies resulted in significant movements with new views of and approaches to the Bible. So called "liberal" scholars in both Protestantism and Catholicism questioned and rejected orthodox views regarding inspiration, Scripture's authority, and hermeneutic. In these circles the notion of the supernatural was usually denied, and the Bible was approached and interpreted like any other literature. Thus, there was no allowance for a role of the Holy Spirit in biblical hermeneutics. American Reformed theologians at Princeton sought to recapture the authority of the Bible by basing that authority upon a verbally inspired inerrant text. Their scholastic approach to the Bible made the study of Scripture a rigid mechanical discipline. Early Princeton theologians posited a role of the Holy Spirit in hermeneutics, but increasing scholastic tendencies eliminated that role in later Princetonians. Neo-orthodox scholars offered an alternative to both liberalism and scholasticism. They ardently affirmed the divine-human character of the Bible and returned faith to a place of priority before reason in their approach to Scripture. Barth's emphasis upon the Spirit's relationship to the "Word of God" included a role of the Holy Spirit in the understanding of Scripture.

CONCLUSION

This historical survey supplies a background for the remainder of this study. It provides a basic understanding of how biblical interpreters since the second century have viewed the Holy Spirit's relationship to hermeneutics. Four important conclusions are drawn from this analysis.

One, most of the major biblical interpreters from the second century to the mid-nineteenth century posited some role of the Holy Spirit in the interpretative process. From the Early Church to the Middle Ages interpreters of the Alexandrian school, the Antiochian school, and the Latin Fathers each held the Holy Spirit's role to be essential. Luther, Calvin, and the other early Reformers along with the later Westminster Divines and Owen all strongly affirmed the Spirit's role in the interpretation of Scripture. Following the Enlightenment, early American Reformed theologians were examples of firm orthodox interpreters who opposed the exclusion of the Holy Spirit by historical-critical scholars. Most recently Barth, with his close identification of the Holy Spirit with the "Word of God," provided a new look at, and emphasis upon, the Spirit's role in understanding Scripture. Finally, one should especially note that interpreters who posited a role of the Holy Spirit in hermeneutics invariably placed faith in priority over reason in their approach to Scripture.

Two, there were times when the Holy Spirit's role was de-emphasized or denied by major hermeneuts. Even as early as the Middle Ages, Aquinas' scholastic methods, and his approach of placing reason in priority over faith, excluded the notion of a role of the Holy Spirit in interpretation. In the Post-Reformation era, Turretin followed Aquinas' scholasticism and placed reason before faith in his approach to the Bible. Consequently, he de-emphasized and greatly restricted the Holy Spirit's role in understanding Scripture. During the Enlightenment, Schleiermacher and others adopted a rationalistic attitude toward Scripture. They held that the Bible must be interpreted according to the same hermeneutical principles as other literature. They saw no role for the Holy Spirit in this process. Finally, the first Princeton theologians, reacting to the Enlightenment, held to traditional methods of interpretation but also adopted Turretin's scholastic approach. Eventually, this approach eliminated the role of the Holy Spirit in their hermeneutics. This indicates that rationalistic and scholastic propensities tended to restrict the relationship of the Holy Spirit to hermeneutics.

Three, those who posited a role of the Spirit in interpretation did not provide extensive descriptions of this work. Specifics regarding "how" the Holy Spirit assisted the interpreter to understand the message were not given. Also, these interpreters did not indicate in concrete, cognitive terms how the understanding given by the Holy Spirit differed from that gained by ordinary means.

Four, most of the major biblical interpreters valued and utilized the common scholarly means of their times. The possible exception to this was Origen and the Alexandrian school. Due to the subjective character of their allegorizing and their emphasis on the "spiritual" sense, they tended to neglect objective methods and the literal sense. However, beginning with the Chrysostom of the Antiochian school, those who posited a role of the Holy Spirit also emphasized the use of ordinary study means. By the middle of the twentieth century the historical-critical method was widely used. Hermeneuts did not see the use of scholarly means as being incompatible with a role of the Holy Spirit. Along with their scholarly efforts they expected the empowering of the Holy Spirit to help them go beyond the "letter" to understand the message of the Spirit. They saw an interpreter's activity of understanding Scripture as a cooperative endeavor between the interpreter and the Holy Spirit.

3

Present Positions

INTRODUCTION

The study of historic positions along with a consideration of the current literature reveals the need for further attention to be given to the issue of the Holy Spirit's role in contemporary hermeneutics. As noted above, biblical scholars of past centuries were often divided in their views, and those who ascribed a role to the Spirit failed to delineate that role adequately. Currently, some scholars want to omit or deny a role of the Holy Spirit in hermeneutics, or they seem uncertain about the matter. Others confidently affirm such a role; but they often fail to delineate it adequately, leaving certain critical questions unanswered. Thus, the issue of the Holy Spirit's relationship to biblical interpretation is characterized by two primary concerns. First, does the Holy Spirit play an essential, authentic role in the hermeneutical process? Second, what major questions are raised when the Spirit is envisioned as having a role in interpretation and how may these questions be answered?

CONTEMPORARY HERMENEUTICS AND THE SPIRIT'S ROLE

Anthony Thiselton suggests a scholar's "approach to the biblical writings is not isolated from broader theological questions about a doctrine of the Word of God."[1] More specifically, among those who hold the Bible to be a special revelation of God to humanity, a particular scholar's position on the Holy Spirit's relationship to hermeneutics depends upon his or her views in two primary areas. One, it depends on the scholar's view regarding the nature of the Bible; and two, it depends on his or her

---

1. Thiselton, *The Two Horizons*, 87.

view regarding the Holy Spirit's present activity in relation to Scripture. Some scholars believe that humanity can understanding the Bible with their ordinary senses and normal reasonable abilities alone. They believe that, in his past activity of giving this special revelation, the Holy Spirit provided it in such a format that humanity is capable of understanding it without the special assistance of the Spirit. Other scholars believe the very nature of this special divine revelation is such that its full understanding is gained only with the Holy Spirit's assistance.

Holy Spirit's Role Denied or Limited

Walter Kaiser represents those scholars who firmly hold the Bible to be God's special revelation, but yet take a position that denies or limits a role of the Holy Spirit in interpretation. He affirms: "It is a fact that [the Bible] is a unique revelation containing supernatural things that no human may aspire to know on his own." Yet Kaiser denies the notion that the Bible calls for a different set of rules or that a person must be spiritually enlightened before he or she can understand Scripture. Rather, he declares: "It is not as if there were two logics and two hermeneutics in the world, one natural and the other spiritual." Kaiser believes the activity of the Holy Spirit is often over pressed in the idea of perspicuity. The Holy Spirit becomes "a magic wand that gives the interpreter not just sufficient and adequate answers for salvation and living but a kind of total knowledge of Scripture."[2]

For Kaiser, the reason a special activity of the Holy Spirit is not appropriate in the interpretative process is precisely because Scripture is special revelation. Scripture is a unique revelation that "God deliberately designed to communicate to human beings what they themselves could or would not know unless they received it from him." That is, in the Bible "God has deliberately decided to accommodate mankind by disclosing himself in our language and according to the mode to which we are accustomed in other literary productions." Thus, Kaiser simply calls for a return to hermeneutical rules and practices that "do not violate what God-given *nature* has taught, *art* has practiced, and *science* has collected and arranged in systems."[3]

2. Kaiser, "Legitimate Hermeneutics," 119, 123, 129.

3. Kaiser, "Legitimate Hermeneutics," 119–21.

The perspective represented by Kaiser has a kinship to the scholastical philosophy and approach of previous ages and decades. Like Aquinas in the Middle Ages, reason is given priority in its approach. Like Turretin in the Post-Reformation era, those in this position are cautious of, if not adverse to, any subjective experience of the Spirit in relation to understanding the Bible. More recently, this stance has its roots in nineteenth century Reformed scholasticism—especially that developed by Warfield; and it continues in twentieth century American fundamentalism.[4] According to Donald Bloesch:

> In this perspective, hermeneutics is considered a scientific discipline abiding by the rules that govern other disciplines of knowledge. According to this view, Scripture yields its meaning to a systematic, inductive analysis and does not necessarily presuppose a faith commitment to be understood.[5]

Bloesch also notes: "In modern fundamentalism . . . the truth of the Bible is held to be directly accessible to human reason."[6]

Hirsch identifies this interpretative position as "positivism."[7] He describes it as follows:

> Under positivism, the mystical distinction between the letter and the spirit is repudiated. The interpreter should ignore the ghost in the verbal machine and simply explain how the verbal machine actually functions. If the rules and canons of construction are made precise, and if the tools of linguistic analysis are sharpened and refined, the problems of interpretation will be resolved in operational procedures.[8]

Millard Erickson observes: "Those who hold this position see an objective quality in the Bible that automatically brings one into contact with

---

4. See Erickson, *Christian Theology*, 251.

5. Bloesch, "A Christological Hermeneutic: Crisis and Conflict in Hermeneutics," 79.

6. Bloesch, *Essentials of Evangelical Theology*, 74.

7. See *EDT*, where *positivism* is described as "a distinctive position in contemporary philosophy which stresses the analysis of language" and places "emphasis on scientific inquiry as the paradigm of human knowledge."

8. Hirsch, "Current Issues in Theory of Interpretation," 302. The reader should note that Hirsch is simply describing this position and not himself ascribing to it.

God."[9] In keeping with scholasticism's philosophical approach, they expect a hermeneutical system that is "clear and definitional in tone."[10]

James Lee is another scholar who, like Kaiser, takes a positivism position. Writing in the broader area of religious epistemology, he notes: "There is no empirical research evidence to suggest that a person learns religion (or even theology) in a way fundamentally different from the basic manner in which he learns any other area of reality." Logically Lee includes the specific activity of "understanding Scripture" in the general activity of "learning." Therefore, he states: "The fact of the matter is that the learner acquires, for example, a knowledge of the Ten Commandments . . . primarily according to the on-going laws of his own human development." Lee rejects what he calls "the Spirit hypothesis." He says: "The Spirit-as-variable fallacy represents a flat rejection of the natural law in any form, and ultimately reduces all human activity . . . to a nihilistic and spooky affair."[11]

G. C. Berkouwer likewise denies a role of the Holy Spirit in understanding Scripture. He limits the Spirit's present activity to that of convincing the reader of the text's authoritative nature. Berkouwer wants to avoid the position that interpretation of Scripture is of "a purely charismatic nature, as mysterious as the blowing of the wind." He believes "spiritualism" in biblical interpretation "relativizes the meaning and function of the written words" and "pneumatic" exegesis "sets charisma in opposition to patient and precise interpretation."[12]

Like Kaiser, Berkouwer emphasizes the idea of "accommodation"—the idea that in Scripture God deliberately accommodates humanity by disclosing himself in human language and thought forms. He suggests:

> All pneumatic exegesis contains a misunderstanding of the fact that the message of salvation does not come to us in a mysterious, cryptic, and unintelligible language of the Spirit, which can only be understood charismatically and pneumatically. The message of salvation comes instead in meaningful human language. Pneumatic exegesis turns Scripture into a mysterious entity, completely inaccessible to everyone lacking the charisma of the Spirit. . . . The biblical text, which comes to us as all other hu-

9. Erickson, *Christian Theology*, 251.

10. German, "Scholasticism," 983.

11. Lee, "The Authentic Source of Religious Instruction," 137, 196.

12. Berkouwer, *Holy Scripture*, 49, 110, 137.

man writings do, can therefore only be understood by the general hermeneutical rules applicable to all literature.[13]

Berkouwer insists: "The text speaks within human existence and . . . does not call for a type of pneumatic exegesis, as though something mysterious could take place during hearing and understanding."[14]

Holy Spirit's Role Included and Emphasized

Most scholars, who hold the Bible to be a special revelation of God to humanity, do conceive of the Holy Spirit playing an essential, authentic role in the hermeneutical process. Thiselton writes:

> If the model of the Holy Spirit's work that is in use approximates to a "ghost in the machine" model, then it is conceivable that a scholar might take the view that the Holy Spirit is "excluded" from "any role in the hermeneutical process." However, the majority of writers in the main-stream of Biblical studies . . . would see the Spirit as operating through the processes of human enquiry.[15]

PROTESTANT SCHOLARS

Carl F. H. Henry is one of the leading Protestant scholars who emphasize the role of the Holy Spirit in interpretation.[16] He rejects the above scholastical approach with its positivistic tendencies. He objects that this approach, with its emphasis on accommodation and Scripture's clarity, appears "prematurely to close the hermeneutical circle in which both the Spirit's inspiration and interpretation are necessary and integral to each other." Henry writes: "The transcendent Spirit of God . . . remains no less active in . . . interpretation of Scripture than in its original inspiration."[17]

In keeping with Reformation doctrine, "Protestant orthodoxy insists that to fully understand Scripture one must be aided by the Spirit."[18] Other representative Protestant scholars include Clark Pinnock who

13. Ibid., 112.

14. Ibid., 118.

15. Anthony C. Thiselton, personal correspondence with John W. Wyckoff, 30 March 1989, letter in the hand of John W. Wyckoff, Waxahachie, TX.

16. See Patterson, *Carl F. H. Henry*, 9, 18, 121, 126.

17. Henry, *God Who Speaks and Shows*, 256, 258.

18. Ibid., 258.

holds: "As the Author of Scripture, the Spirit is its best Interpreter, and he assists our interpretation in a special sense."[19] Bernard Ramm agrees that "an interpreter must have the same Spirit who inspired the Bible as the *sine qua non* for interpreting the Bible."[20] Erickson briefly states three basic views. He then adopts the one which "contends that there is an internal working of the Holy Spirit, illumining the understanding of the hearer or reader of the Bible, bringing about comprehension of its meaning."[21] Likewise, Bloesch also contends: "Apart from the work of the Spirit, the . . . transcendent truth of Scripture cannot be perceived."[22] A final example is Thomas F. Torrance who affirms that through the Scripture, the Spirit of Truth "articulates God's Word within our understanding [and] leads us into all truth."[23]

ROMAN CATHOLIC SCHOLARS

In Roman Catholic scholarship, clear statements concerning the role of the Holy Spirit in interpretation are less frequent but nevertheless present. Such a role is often implied rather than explicitly stated.[24] For example, Terence Keegan briefly notes the idea of the reader being "guided by the light of the Holy Spirit." Later he discusses 2 Cor 3:15. He states that in contrast to Old Testament and intertestamental times, believers can now read and understand Moses because "the veil has been removed by the Spirit that makes them able to read what the Spirit wants them to read in these books." Keegan sees a close relation between the church, the Scripture, and the Spirit. He suggests Scripture cannot be properly understood apart from the church and the Holy Spirit.[25]

Also, at present there is renewed discussion of the idea of "the *sensus plenior*" which literally means "the fuller sense." Raymond Edward Brown defines it as "that additional, deeper meaning, intended by God

---

19. Pinnock, *Biblical Revelation: The Foundation of Christian Theology*, 215.

20. Ramm, *Protestant Biblical Interpretation*, 12.

21. Erickson, *Christian Theology*, 246–47.

22. Bloesch, *Essentials of Evangelical Theology*, 65.

23. Torrance, *God and Rationality*, 174, 181.

24. See Hoffman, "Inspiration, Normativeness, Canonicity, and the Unique Sacred Character of the Bible," 458.

25. Keegan, *Interpreting the Bible*, 19, 151, 161. Keegan is a member of the Dominican Order.

but not clearly intended by the human author."[26] Renewed discussion of the *sensus plenior* concept, which is prominent among Roman Catholic scholars, parallels general Roman Catholic interest in the work of the Holy Spirit since Vatican II. John Breck observes: "Since the Second Vatican Council, Catholic theologians have gone far toward rediscovering the 'hermeneutic function' of the Holy Spirit."[27]

The concept of *sensus plenior* lends itself to the idea of a role of the Holy Spirit in understanding the full sense of Scripture. This concept emphasizes the belief that God is the ultimate author of Scripture. It also highlights the need for faith in interpreting Scripture. In an article dealing with the *sensus plenior*, Sandra Schneiders, of the Jesuit School of Theology at Berkley, writes: "The faith of the exegete becomes integral to the work of exegesis."[28] This notion of faith implies a Divine activity of the Holy Spirit when the reader seeks to understand Scripture. William LaSor explains that since God is Spirit humanity's relationship with him is a spiritual relationship. Therefore, "there is a spiritual significance in the Scripture. It is for this reason that God's people have referred to the Scripture as God's Word, and have always searched it for spiritual truth." He adds that "to discover the spiritual meaning involves more than grammatico-historical exegesis."[29] Thus, James Wood concludes: "The Plenary Sense is dependent on the work of the Holy Spirit, made available through the teaching office of the church, or through the intuition of faith."[30]

Why Posit a Role of the Spirit in Hermeneutics

The question might be asked: Why do scholars, both Protestant and Roman Catholic, posit a role of the Holy Spirit in the hermeneutical process? A review of the literature reveals various aspects of the answer to this question.

HUMANITY'S SIN BLINDNESS

Some scholars hold that humanity is hindered in understanding the Bible because of their fall into sin. "At our own human level, we are all sinners,

---

26. Brown, *The Sensus Plenior of Sacred Scripture*, 92.

27. Breck, "Exegesis and Interpretation," 84.

28. Schneiders, "Faith, Hermeneutics, and the Literal Sense of Scripture," 729.

29. LaSor, "Prophecy, Inspiration, and *Sensus Plenior*," 52.

30. Wood, *The Interpretation of the Bible*, 163.

with alienated hearts and darkened minds."[31] This viewpoint emphasizes the detrimental effects of sin upon man's noetic powers. "The Bible witnesses in numerous and emphatic ways to this encumbrance of human understanding, particularly with regard to spiritual matters," Erickson says.[32] According to Walter Dunnett the illuminating work of the Holy Spirit is "a necessary work due to the effects of sin upon our beings. Without it the intended meaning of many biblical statements will be distorted or even missed completely in our study of Scripture."[33]

HUMANITY'S FINITUDE

More scholars, however, see humanity's hindrance in understanding Scripture as being primarily due to his finitude in relation to God's infinitude. There is an inherent lack in humanity's ability to comprehend revelation because of the ontological difference between humanity and God. In the truth of a transcendent God, there is a transcendent quality that is beyond humanity's natural comprehension. These scholars may recognize the operation of accommodation in the Holy Spirit's previous activity of inspiration when the written Word was being produced. Yet, they point out: "God is transcendent; he goes beyond our categories of understanding. He can never be fully grasped within our finite concepts or by our human vocabulary."[34]

Even in the area of humanity's attempts to communicate concerning "ordinary" things, scholars commonly recognize that human languages are often pressed to their limits. The best linguistic medium reaches a point at which it is inadequate to express fully the author's conceptions and thoughts. Often, that which one desires to communicate ultimately transcends the available linguistic medium. Robert W. Funk notes: "When language is pressed to its limits, it is discovered . . . that it is more than sentences composed of subject and predicate." He suggests that the authentic poet is an example of one who presses the limits of language. The authentic poet crosses "the frontier of conventional parlance into uncharted linguistic terrain . . . to articulate for himself that which has not yet come to expression."[35] Likewise, in a fashion similar to

31. Bromiley, "The Interpretation of the Bible," 1:65.
32. Erickson, *Christian Theology*, 247.
33. Dunnett, *The Interpretation of Holy Scripture*, 80.
34. Erickson, *Christian Theology*, 247.
35. Funk, *Language, Hermeneutic, and the Word of God*, 2.

the authentic poet, the words of the inspired prophets and apostles are also written to articulate truth that transcends the linguistic medium. Contrary to the positivist, "the intuitionist must therefore be right," Hirsch concludes, "to insist on transcending the letter."[36]

In the case of the biblical writings, transcending the linguistic medium is of a realm that is yet beyond that which ordinarily attends to communication with language. That is, especially in Scripture, "we are up against what is transcendent to thought and always reaches beyond what we are able to specify," as Torrance says. "This is knowledge with a transcendence in form and an indefinite range of enlightenment beyond anything else in our experience."[37] James Smart expresses a similar idea. He writes:

> It must be recognized that the Biblical records, because they have to do with God and with the purposes of God for humanity through all the ages, constantly point to realities that are far beyond the conscious grasp of any human being. The writers themselves are conscious of the mysterious depths of the word that comes to them out of the unseen and that they speak as best they can.[38]

Alan Richardson notes that "modern science has gradually helped us to see more clearly that what is revealed in the Bible is not . . . any kind of truth which can be investigated or verified by scientific method." He adds: "Scientific knowledge can describe one aspect of the relation between the individual and the universe, but it is not the most important aspect." In Scripture, "there is a knowledge of our 'existence' that is not reached by the processes and methods of objective-scientific thinking."[39] In Scripture, the finite human interpreter is dealing with the supreme truth and wisdom of the infinite God.

The Spirit's Epistemological Role

How is it, then, that a finite human interpreter can come to understand the infinite truth in Scripture given by the transcendent God? Ramm answers: "The Eternal Spirit creates a bridge from his infinitude to the

---

36. Hirsch, "Current Issues," 301.

37. Torrance, *God and Rationality*, 169, 170.

38. Smart, *The Interpretation of Scripture*, 35.

39. Richardson, *The Bible in the Age of Science*, 12, 102, 104.

finitude of man."[40] This raises the question of the epistemological relevance of the Holy Spirit. Torrance asks: "'Is it meaningful to speak of the epistemology of the Spirit?' Yes, for 'we do not have any knowledge of God apart from the Spirit, for God is Spirit and we know him in truth as we know him in the Spirit.'" With the Word, of which Scripture is the written form, the Holy Spirit "breaks through the distance between the creature and the Creator."[41] Torrance concludes:

> How is it that human beings, by means of human language, have come to speak of what is ineffable? How can we through human words which are correlated to created realities speak truly of the Supreme Being who transcends them altogether? This is what takes place through the operation of the Holy Spirit who relates the divine being to our forms of thought and speech and realizes the relation of our forms of thought and speech to the truth of God—what cannot be done by our thinking or stating is done by his *action* as Spirit.[42]

Ramsey's work, *Models for Divine Activity*, provides insights about the epistemological relevance of the Spirit. His study of *ruach* in the Old Testament and *pneuma* in New Testament shows that "Spirit" is the primary model for God's activity. "*Spirit is a noun* whose logical tradition is more reliably a verb: *being active, God-active.*" Ian T. Ramsey concludes then that "discourse about the Spirit is a way of being articulate about the activity of God."[43] Spirit-illumination of Scripture is the God activity of making Scripture understandable and relevant to the reader in his or her human reality.

The epistemological relevance of the Holy Spirit to Scripture means the transcendent God is immanently active in making his Word know to contemporary human beings. What Wolfhart Pannenberg says about the concept of "spirit" relative to God's transcendence and immanence in general is thus applicable in the specific case of Scripture. "The idea of spirit allows us to do justice to the transcendence of God and at the same time to explain his immanence in his creation."[44] In the case of Scripture

---

40. Ramm, *The Witness of the Spirit*, 31.

41. Torrance, *God and Rationality*, 165, 173.

42. Ibid., 186.

43. Ramsey, *Models for Divine Activity*, 2, 7–14.

44. Pannenberg, "The Working of the Spirit in the Creation and in the People of God," 21.

this means that the linguistic media, instead of remaining opaque, by the Spirit-activity of God become "transparent frames of signification."[45] It also means that the ancient inscribed Word becomes understandable and relevant in humanity's present situation. Carl Braaten writes:

> It is finally the Spirit . . . who "merges the horizons" of the Biblical text and contemporary existence: . . . it is the Spirit who spans the wide chasm of the centuries between Biblical *Heilsgeschichte* and present-day history. In the last analysis, a hermeneutic without the Pentecostal principle is a key that cannot unlock the mystery of God's revelation in Scripture.[46]

ILLUMINATION'S RELATIONSHIP TO INSPIRATION

Many scholars believe the epistemological relevance of the Holy Spirit—his present illumination role in the hermeneutical process—is indicated by and logically follows from the concept of Spirit-inspiration of Scripture. This is in keeping with the close relationship seen between the Holy Spirit and the revelatory Word. Pinnock writes:

> The objective, divine revelation is accompanied by a subjective divine Revealer; the Word *and* the Spirit, a duality not to be disregarded. The Spirit *speaks* in Scripture. He is responsible for *two* miracles in regard to it: the miracle of inspiration by which revelation was infallibly recorded, and the miracle of illumination by which the book is understood and believed.[47]

Torrance emphasizes the relationship of the Spirit to the media of revelation. Biblical revelation is the result of God's endeavor to use the linguistic medium of inter-human communication to communicate himself to humanity. Scripture was brought forth by "the inspiration of the Holy Spirit and appointed as the medium which he continues to use in the revelation of God to man."[48] Geoffrey Bromiley believes the idea of "God-breathed" in the Bible implies "proper interpretation has to be in the Holy Spirit."[49] Likewise, Peter Stuhlmacher writes: "The *theopneustia* in Scripture means that only an interpretation which is

45. Torrance, *God and Rationality*, 192.

46. Braaten, *History and Hermeneutics*, 157.

47. Pinnock, *Biblical Revelation*, 216.

48. Torrance, *God and Rationality*, 184.

49. Bromiley, "Interpretation of the Bible," 78.

borne by the Holy Spirit can really determine and pass on the inspired testimony of Scripture."[50]

Summary

This study shows that scholars who consider the Bible to be a special revelation of God are divided on the idea of a role of the Holy Spirit in the hermeneutical process. In the view of some, the role of the Spirit is denied or greatly limited. Others posit such a role and emphasize the importance of the Spirit's present function in gaining understanding of Scripture.

Those who deny or greatly limit the Holy Spirit's role in hermeneutics emphasize the concept of "accommodation" and humanity's ordinary abilities to learn and understand. They believe that in the activity of inspiration God accommodated mankind by disclosing his Truth in human language and thought forms. This detail of accommodation is sufficient to the extent that understanding of Scripture occurs the same way as the understanding of other ancient literature. The reader does not need special spiritual enlightenment in order to interpret Scripture properly.

Those who posit a role of the Holy Spirit in interpretation believe his active participation is necessary because of humanity's sin blindness and/or finitude. They suggest the Spirit's participation in the former activity of inspiration indicates his present participation in illumination. These scholars contend the Holy Spirit's epistemological relevance to Scripture enables finite humanity to understand and receive God's transcendent message. Without the Spirit's enlightenment, the reader would not be able to fully comprehend the Supreme Truth of Scripture.

Thus, although the role of the Holy Spirit in interpretation is admittedly an intangible component, many scholars confidently affirm that his active participation is essential and logical. The Holy Spirit's work in the interpreter's mind is "an issue which falls outside the area of scientific analysis, but is nevertheless of utmost importance in the interpretation of Scripture," C. Hassell Bullock contends.[51]

---

50. Stuhlmacher, "Ex Auditu and the Theological Interpretation of Holy Scripture," 5.
51. Bullock, "Introduction: Interpreting the Bible," 14.

ISSUES RELATED TO THE HOLY SPIRIT'S ROLE

Several significant questions are raised by the position that posits a role of the Holy Spirit in the hermeneutical process. What is the content and nature of the message that the Spirit helps one to understand? How is the Holy Spirit's role in hermeneutics to be conceptualized? What is the human role in interpretation when the Holy Spirit is involved? Who can be co-interpreters with the Holy Spirit; can any and all persons participate?

The issues related to the Holy Spirit's role in understanding Scripture are not only significant, they are enigmatic. Scholars who posit a role of the Holy Spirit in hermeneutics quickly recognize the intangibility and mystery of this activity. Pannenberg's observation is especially relevant here. "It is rather hard to find out what kind of reality one is talking about in referring to the Holy Spirit."[52] Thus, scholars generally find these issues quite difficult to address—elusive to conceptualization and articulation. No wonder J. I. Packer finds that "most evangelical textbooks on interpreting Scripture say little or nothing about the Holy Spirit."[53]

Since it is of a realm beyond and is difficult to address, does positing a role of the Holy Spirit in understanding Scripture doom the would be interpreter to hermeneutical nihilism? No, for these scholars contend that although the Spirit's activity is a mystery it is nevertheless real and not necessarily beyond conceptualization. In fact, Ramm suggests: "The intangibility of the work of the Spirit might be far more real than all the scientific procedures applied to the text."[54]

Torrance addresses the question of whether or not the activity of the Holy Spirit can be conceptualized? He acknowledges that human forms of thought and language are limited in their ability to picture the reality of the invisible God. One's thoughts about the activity of the Holy Spirit lead one "far beyond the imaginable." Theology makes immense demands upon one's mental powers; and human language falls short in picturing the theological concepts and realities to which scholars often desire to refer. The conceptual relation they involve lies beyond the range of the imaginable; however, "this does not invalidate the concepts," Torrance says. "Indeed this is the only kind of conceptual relation that would be

---

52. Pannenberg, "Working of the Spirit," 13.

53. Packer, "Infallible Scripture and the Role of Hermeneutics," 347.

54. See Ramm, "Hermeneutics," 104.

appropriate to God." He contends: "It does not follow from the fact that we are unable to give a precise conceptual definition of the reality of God that it cannot be conceptually grasped."[55] Therefore, Torrance and others agree with Bullock who insists: "Admittedly this is an elusive element in hermeneutics. Yet those who believe in the authority of the Bible are compelled to deal with this issue in any study of interpretation."[56]

Content and Nature of the Illuminated Message

If the Holy Spirit assists the reader in understanding Scripture, one of the first questions to be raised is, how does the message differ from that understood by ordinary means? Is there some distinctive difference in its content and nature? If so, how is the illuminated message to be described?

MEANING BEYOND THE WRITER'S UNDERSTANDING

Scholars who posit a role of the Holy Spirit in hermeneutics also usually believe that the understanding that he brings by illumination may include nuances not always understood by the writers themselves. That is, they believe the text may include a meaning not apparently intended by the writer but seen to be intended by God. Arden Autry observes that "the language of the Bible does seem to have a dynamic quality not always exhausted by the author's original intention."[57] Schneiders holds that the Scripture text includes meaning "beyond the explicit concern of the human author."[58] David Stacey says that there is "a deeper intent not always understood by the writers."[59]

The notion that the text can have meaning not understood by the writer raises a question. What, if any, is the relationship between present-day readers' understanding of the text and the writers' understanding or intention? Does the Holy Spirit convey meaning apart from or out of conformity to the writers' intentions? Among scholars there are two schools of thought.

One school holds that contemporary understanding of the text is not bound or governed in any way by the writer's perceptions. The text

55. Torrance, *God and Rationality*, 22–23.

56. Bullock, "Introduction: Interpreting the Bible," 14–15.

57. Autry, "The Five Dimensions of Hermeneutics," 10.

58. Schneiders, "Faith, Hermeneutics, and the Literal Sense," 725.

59. Stacey, *Interpreting the Bible*, 5–7.

mysteriously speaks on its own without reference to the writer's intention. The interpreter may expect to discover meaning totally apart from what the writers intended.

"Structuralism" is a recent interpretive methodology that takes the view that the writer's original intention is not important. This method studies the biblical text with the belief that therein there exist deep structures that display atemporal and transcultural patterns of thought and experience. These deep structures exhibit uniformity and embody meaning that transcend time and space. Writers do not produce the meaning of their texts so much as do the deep structures that, for the most part, are not consciously recognized. Therefore, much of the meaning effect of a literary work is found in the deep structures that lie outside the intention of the writer.[60]

"The New Hermeneutic" is another methodology in which the meaning of the text is not bound or governed by the writer's original intention. Following Rudolf Bultmann, Ernst Fuchs and Gerhard Ebeling develop Martin Heidegger's hermeneutical idea that language mysteriously speaks in semantic autonomy independent of the writer's designs.[61] Contemporary readings of the text cannot be bound by the writer's understanding. Hans-Georg Gadamer expresses this view when he writes: "The very idea of a definitive interpretation seems to be intrinsically contradictory. Interpretation is always on the way." More important than the writer's original meaning is the "event" when "the word of scripture addresses us." In this "event" the interpreter not only interprets but is in turn also himself interpreted by the text.[62]

There is a second school of thought concerning the relationship of present-day meaning to the writer's intention. In this second perspective, both the writer's original understanding and the meaning intended by God are held to be important. Biblical interpretation appropriately begins with determining the writer's original meaning, but it then moves on to discover what God may intend for Scripture to mean to present-day readers. Hirsch writes twenty-three pages "in defense of the author"

60. Keegan, *Interpreting the Bible*, 43–46, 171. For complete discussion of Structuralism, the reader should see Patte, *What Is Structural Exegesis?*

61. Gruenler, "The New Hermeneutic," 763–65; Hirsch, *Validity*, 1. For more extensive discussion of the New Hermeneutic, see Robinson and Cobb, *New Frontiers in Theology*.

62. Gadamer, *Reason in the Age of Science*, 105; Gadamer, *Truth and Method*, 297.

against those who would ignore or contradict the writer's originally intended meaning.[63] Daniel J. Harrington uses nine chapters in *Interpreting the New Testament: A Practical Guide* to show how to discover "as far as possible what the text meant to its original audience and in its original historical setting."[64] Henry notes: "Emphasis on the inspired writer's intention as the key to the meaning of Scripture has become highly important in recent decades when post-Bultmannians have emphasized, instead, the interpreter's creative contribution to meaning."[65]

Recognizing the validity of a sense beyond the writer's understanding, these same interpreters cited above also emphasize the importance of discovering the meaning of the text in the contemporary situation. Hirsch says, "It is not possible to mean what one does not mean"; nevertheless, he allows, "It is very possible to mean what one is not conscious of meaning."[66] To his explanation of how to ascertain the original meaning, Harrington adds:

> Nevertheless, few people who read the Scriptures are satisfied with merely determining what the text meant in antiquity. Most of us come to the Scriptures with the assumption that we will find there something significant for the way we live our lives and the way we think about ultimate realities.[67]

Henry cautions that while the writer's intention is the key to Scripture's meaning, "it must not be assumed . . . that the human author necessarily is aware of the full meaning of his message. The meaning of the text may also bear nuances of which the writer is unaware."[68]

The God-intended meaning, which the writer may or may not have fully understood, is ultimately the most significant meaning to present-day readers. Again, as Harrington notes, "Few people who read the Scriptures are satisfied with merely determining what the text meant in antiquity." They expect to gain "spiritual insights" which are significant

---

63. Hirsch, *Validity in Interpretation*, 1–23.

64. Harrington, *Interpreting the New Testament*, 124.

65. Henry, *God Who Speaks and Shows*, 281.

66. Hirsch, *Validity*, 22. Later, Hirsch adds: "The human author's willed meaning can always go beyond what he consciously intended so long as it remains within his willed type," 126.

67. Harrington, *Interpreting the New Testament*, 126.

68. Henry, *God Who Speaks and Shows*, 281.

for the ultimate realities of their present lives.[69] Therefore, to deny the reality and validity of God-intended meaning besides what the writers original understanding, would be to effectively silence the Bible. Smart contends:

> To deny the possibility of these deeper implications of the text would be to deny that the word of the prophet is really the word of a God whose purpose comprehends the whole of human history; in short, it would be to deny the mystery of Scripture and to reduce all its words to no more than human words.[70]

In other words, the contents of Scripture are "special revelation" which the writers may or may not have fully understood in their times; and it is the Holy Spirit who illuminates and brings understanding of this revelation to the Spirit-enlightened reader.

No New Revelations

When the Spirit illuminates the interpreter, enabling him or her to gain fresh insight into the meaning of the text—insight that even the writer may not have had—this does not include new revelations. Bloesch believes that God's "truth would remain buried in the past unless the Spirit were active now bringing it to light." He adds, however, "What the Spirit reveals is not a new word but the truth already proclaimed in Holy Scripture."[71] Henry argues against Barth's idea that illumination is simply a continuation of inspiration. Henry is also concerned about extreme pentecostals or charismatics who appeal to fresh revelations given by the Spirit beyond the prophetic-apostolic Word. "While the Spirit retains an exposing ministry within the church, that role . . . does not involve the communication of new truths as was the case in the inspiration of the biblical autographs," Henry says. Illumination is not "a contemporary impartation of new or original revelation, but rather the Spirit's enlivening to us individually of the objectively given special biblical revelation."[72]

Other scholars (including leading pentecostals) who advocate an illumination doctrine, share Henry's concern about all manner of new

---

69. Harrington, *Interpreting the New Testament*, 126.

70. Smart, *Interpretation of Scripture*, 36.

71. Bloesch, "The Sword of the Spirit," 72.

72. Henry, *God Who Speaks and Shows*, 256–66, 275, 283–84.

revelations and private interpretations. Gordon Fee chides: "We cannot make [Scripture] mean anything that pleases us, and then give the Holy Spirit 'credit' for it."[73] Likewise, Mark McLean warns against "personal revelation of the Holy Spirit to the individual which transcends the plain sense of the written canonical text."[74] There is a genuine difference between the Spirit's work of illuminating the divinely intended meaning, on the one hand; and the intuitive opinions and additions of various so-called interpreters, on the other hand.[75]

The Holy Spirit can be expected not to contradict himself by giving "private interpretations" which are out-of-character with the original intent that he inspired. The interpreter is indebted to the Reformation for restoring the right of private interpretation. However, George Montaque concludes: "Private interpretation does not have the guarantee of divine authority or of being inspired by the Holy Spirit." He believes the writer of 2 Pet 1:20–21 is coping with a kind of "pneumaticism gone rampant" in the first century.[76] Now, as in the first century, the right of private interpretation has its limitations. It means readers and listeners should not simply assume that the interpretations of others are correct. However, it does not mean that, even if one claims illumination of the Holy Spirit, his or her own interpretations are guaranteed to be any more correct.[77]

Thus, scholars recognize the need for a safeguard against out-of-character intuitive opinions while at the same time allowing the Spirit to function as illuminator of the text. Adequate appreciation of the *communal character* of biblical interpretation is recognized as such a safeguard against private misinterpretations. Breck suggests that contemporary interpreters should follow in the tradition of successful and effective Christian hermeneutes of past centuries. In doing so they will see the activity of scriptural interpretation "not as a personal exercise undertaken on their own authority, but *under the continued guidance of the Spirit within the ecclesial community*."[78] The Spirit's activity of illumination may be expected to function "within the believing community," Fred H. Klooster says. "The Holy Spirit works in individual persons, but

73. Fee and Stuart, *How to Read the Bible for all Its Worth*, 26.

74. McLean, "Toward a Pentecostal Hermeneutic," 36.

75. See Virkler, *Hermeneutics*, 30–31.

76. Montague, *The Holy Spirit*, 315–16.

77. Autry, "Five Dimensions of Hermeneutics," 19–20.

78. Breck, "Exegesis and Interpretation," 90.

his work is not individualistic."[79] Pinnock aptly states: "The interpreter is not a solo virtuoso but the member of a [sic] interpreting team and fellowship that collectively seeks to know the mind of God for the whole of life."[80]

In his article on "The Five Dimensions of Hermeneutics," Autry discusses "Community" as the fifth necessary dimension. He suggests acknowledgment of this dimension means at least two things: biblical interpretation is a community task; and private interpretation should be open to be informed by the understanding of others. Autry recognizes the subjectivity inherent in interacting with the Holy Spirit and the text. He suggests that personal experience related to interpretation "is best kept on track not simply through comparison with objective data in the text (important as that is) but also through the sharing of experiences in a community of believers." One's personal understanding of Scripture can be enriched instead of impoverished if the role of the Christian community is adequately appreciated and received.[81]

ULTRACOGNITIVE UNDERSTANDING

Those who posit a role of the Holy Spirit in hermeneutics believe he brings an understanding that is beyond the cognitive level gained by normal human understanding of the linguistic media. "Interpretation of Scripture involves much more than head-knowledge or the gaining of information, historical or other."[82] Illumination takes the reader beyond ordinary human comprehension to the "Supreme Truth" of Scripture, as Torrance calls it. He asserts that when the writers produced the scriptural forms of discourse inspired by the Spirit they simply proclaimed more than they could communicate with the linguistic media.[83] Howard M. Ervin, discussing the understanding one gains by the Holy Spirit's illumination, writes:

79. Klooster, "The Role of the Holy Spirit in the Hermeneutic Process," 465.

80. Pinnock, *The Scripture Principle*, 221.

81. Autry, "Five Dimensions of Hermeneutics," 19–22. What Torrance says concerning theological statements can also be said about interpretations of Scripture. "The more ecumenical they are, i.e., the more they are formulated within the openness of the members of the whole Community to one another before God, the more likely they are to escape distortion through false in-turned subjectivity." Torrance, *God and Rationality*, 190.

82. Klooster, "Role of the Holy Spirit," 462.

83. Torrance, *God and Rationality*, 148–49.

[Scripture] is a word for which, in fact, there is no hermeneutic unless and until the divine *hermeneutes* (the Holy Spirit) mediates an understanding. . . . Thus the hearing and understanding of the word is qualitatively more than an exercise in semantics. It is theological (*theos-logos*) communication in its deepest ontological context. . . . It is not simply grasping the kerygma cognitively.[84]

Torrance goes on to discuss the "Supreme Truth" content of Scripture and the essential role of the Holy Spirit in bringing it to humanity's understanding. He writes:

The biblical statements and all the forms of signification in thought and speech they involve can be interpreted in their human reference as expressing the attitudes and thoughts and the time-conditioned and space-conditioned limitations of their human authors, and when left to themselves can only be interpreted in that way. That is to say, we interpret them only in terms of their mediate and not their ultimate objectivity in God's own self-revelation. Now this is precisely where the activity of the Holy Spirit comes in . . . and makes us capable of knowing him beyond ourselves.

Torrance concludes that one who handles Scripture must understand the biblical statements not merely as cognitive linguistic forms and logical facts but as expressions of "the Supreme Truth."[85]

The understanding one gains by the Holy Spirit's illumination is beyond the ordinary cognitive level because it pertains to the area of "subjective knowledge." Bloesch calls this the "revelatory meaning" of the text that cannot be procured by any ordinary technique.[86] As seen in later discussion herein, diligent human efforts and scholarly techniques are essential; but, in themselves, these fall short of revealing the divine mysteries which lie beyond ordinary cognition. Ervin notes that "linguistic, literary and historical analysis are indispensable as a first step to an understanding of the Scripture. . . . But rationality by itself is inadequate for the task of interpreting the words of Scripture."[87] Rationality by itself is inadequate for the task because the "revelatory meaning" belongs to

---

84. Ervin, "Hermeneutics: A Pentecostal Option," 16–17.

85. Torrance, *God and Rationality*, 185–86.

86. Bloesch, "A Christological Hermeneutic," 100.

87. Ervin, "Hermeneutics," 18.

a reality unreached by the processes and methods of objective-scientific inquiry. It belongs to the divine dimension of reality with which the historical-critical method is unable to deal.[88] The understanding one gains by enlightenment of the Holy Spirit is the transcendent, "spiritual meaning" intended by God.

The "Supreme Truth" of Scripture—its "spiritual meaning"—being in the realm of subjective knowledge, is gained only when the reader personally experiences the reality of God. Charles Wood, in his article, "Finding the Life of the Text," notes the limitation of mere words and verbal explanation; he concludes one knows the text only through experience in the Spirit.[89] The knowledge that the Holy Spirit brings, then, is *experiential* knowledge. Autry identifies this as "knowledge *of* [my emphasis] (not simply about) God." He cautions that subjective experience cannot be made a prerequisite for biblical hermeneutics; but, "experiences of encounter with transcendence, . . . must be seen as the goal of hermeneutics."[90] Klooster refers to the knowledge gained in experience with the Holy Spirit simply as "heart-understanding"—the richly personal dimension one experiences in the I-thou relationship with God. He suggests that the heart-understanding which comes in the experience of regeneration is "the most radical form of illumination one experiences."[91] The experiential aspect of knowledge and the significance of the Spirit's role are seen in Nash's statement. "God's Revelation must become alive and dynamic in the present experience of the believer, through the action of the Holy Spirit."[92]

Scholars point out that Paul makes a distinction between cognitive understanding and spiritual understanding in his writings. In 2 Cor 3:6 this distinction is between the "letter" that kills and the "Spirit" which gives life. The Holy Spirit imparts to the text its dynamic, life-giving quality. The living text is the text as understood in the Spirit. In 1 Cor 2:7–13 Paul writes about what the "spiritual" (*pneumatikos*) person can "know" (*ginosko*) and what the "natural" (*psychikos*) person cannot "know" (*ginosko*). Fuller and Autry agree that in this passage *ginosko* must mean

---

88. See Richardson, *The Bible in the Age of Science*, 101–4; LaSor, "Prophecy, Inspiration, and *Sensus Plenior*," 52–53; and Hasel, *New Testament Theology*, 209–11.

89. Wood, "Finding the Life of a Text," 102–4.

90. Autry, "Five Dimensions of Hermeneutics," 15–18.

91. Klooster, "Role of the Holy Spirit," 454–57, 461–63.

92. Nash, *The Word of God and the Mind of Man*, 41.

more than to have cognition or understanding in the ordinary sense. Otherwise Paul would be saying that biblical statements are in no sense intelligible to the "natural" person. What the "spiritual" person "knows" that the "natural" person "does not know," is not just ordinary, cognitive information but rather spiritual reality—"God's wisdom in a mystery," which is "hidden wisdom" until it is revealed and taught by the Holy Spirit.[93]

ULTIMATE ILLUMINATION

If that which the Holy Spirit makes known is "God's wisdom in a mystery," then, the ultimate content of the illuminated message is Christ—his person and his work. For the ultimate wisdom of God—the ultimate revelation of God—is none other than Jesus Christ himself. Pinnock expresses the consensus view. "The *purpose* of Scripture is identical with the purpose of revelation itself: to witness to Jesus as the Christ. . . . It is at heart Christocentric. He is the hub of its message."[94]

When the reader truly knows the meaning of Scripture, what he or she understands is God's message in and through Jesus Christ. Robert L. Saucy writes: "Since Christ is the theme of Scripture, the Holy Spirit illumines Scripture in such a way as to reveal him in all of his glory." He adds: "A 'full assurance of understanding' which comes only by the Spirit results 'in a true knowledge of God's mystery, that is, Christ himself' (Col. 2:2)."[95] Though the media of Scripture are forms of thought and speech common to humanity, Christ is "God's exclusive language to us," Torrance says. Revelational truth is the unveiling of what is hidden, the manifestation of the divine Reality. The Holy Spirit is called the Spirit of Truth because Christ is the Truth and He bears witness to Christ. That is, to know the revelation of God in Scripture is to know more than the linguistic forms of thought and speech; it is to know the being of God in Christ. "Apart from the Spirit we would not break through to [Christ], or rather the divine being would not break through to us in his reality as being and thus in His distinction from our thought and speech of him."[96]

---

93. Fuller, "The Holy Spirit's Role in Biblical Interpretation," 191–92; Autry, "The Spiritual Man and Understanding," 2–3, 10–11.

94. Pinnock, *Biblical Revelation*, 36.

95. Saucy, *The Bible: Breathed from God*, 106, 110.

96. Torrance, *God and Rationality*, 151, 167.

How the Spirit Illuminates the Message

Distinguishing and describing the content and nature of the illuminated message is difficult enough. Conceptualizing and articulating *how* the Spirit brings enlightened understanding to the mind of the reader is even more difficult. Scholars like Klooster readily admit: "The task of analyzing the precise nature of the Spirit's illumination is extremely difficult. The difficulty is analogous to that of attempting to describe the exact nature of the process of inspiration."[97] Ramm concedes that how the Holy Spirit illuminates is a mystery. "We know nothing concretely or empirically about such an act."[98] Henry notes: "If we ask how the Holy Spirit illumines us, we must readily acknowledge that Scripture does not supply much data about the *how* of inspiration or illumination."[99]

Although the task is difficult, making immense demands upon one's mental powers, it does not follow that the *how* of the Holy Spirit's activity in hermeneutics cannot be conceptualized and articulated at all. True, one's thoughts about the activity of the Holy Spirit lead one far beyond the imaginable. Yet, as Torrance shows this does not doom theologians to nihilistic indefinite, non-conceptual envisaging.[100] Rather, at this point in the discussion the use of metaphors and models becomes entirely natural and extremely important.

METAPHORS

Scholars, seeking to conceptualize and articulate *how* the Spirit brings about understanding of Scriptural truth, use various metaphors— comparisons by direct assertion. A metaphor that immediately comes to mind is one that is inherent in the term "illumination." This term is itself a metaphorical expression of the Holy Spirit's activity in effecting understanding. It pictures the Spirit as one who "shines light" in an otherwise darkened area. Scripture itself suggests this metaphor. For example, in Eph 1:18 the writer prays that the "eyes" of his readers' hearts may be "enlightened" so that they may know certain things of God. Here, E. K. Simpson suggests that "the illumination he [the Spirit] desiderates is inward, not dependent on the senses or even the mental activities, so

---

97. Klooster, "Role of the Holy Spirit," 452.

98. Ramm, *Witness of the Spirit*, 73.

99. Henry, *God Who Speaks and Shows*, 277.

100. Torrance, *God and Rationality*, 22–23.

much as on the spiritual enlightenment that assimilates divine truth."[101] In 2 Cor 4:6, the writer states: "For God, who said, 'Light shall shine out of darkness,' is the One who has shone in our hearts to give the light of the knowledge of the glory of God in the face of Christ." Philip Hughes notes that the term "heart" means the Holy Spirit shines true knowledge (*gnosis*) into "the centre of man's whole being, moral, intellectual, and spiritual."[102]

In the "shining of light" metaphor, the idea is that the Spirit illumines the text being interpreted and/or the mind of the interpreter with a bright light. Humanity's minds are said to be "darkened" by sin and in need of enlightenment. The linguistic media in themselves are "dark and opaque." The Holy Spirit shines divine light to dispel the darkness and shine through the opaqueness.[103]

Scholars make frequent use of this metaphor. For example, Packer sees the Holy Spirit as being the great hermeneut who, by "*enlightening* (my emphasis) us in the work of exegesis, synthesis, and application, actually interprets that [Scripture] in our minds and to our hearts."[104] Bloesch says that the Spirit brings the truth of Scripture "to light in the consciousness of men and women."[105] Torrance uses this metaphor when he writes about the Holy Spirit's activity in relation to the understanding of Scripture. "Apart from this work of the Holy Spirit all forms of revelation remain dark and opaque but in and through his presence they become translucent and transparent."[106]

In another metaphor the Holy Spirit is said to be one who "guides" the reader into truth. This figure comes from John 16:13 where Jesus is cited as saying: "But when he, the Spirit of truth, comes, he will guide you into all truth." A guide is one who leads another through unknown or unfamiliar areas. Thus, the Holy Spirit is portrayed as acting like a scout who is familiar with a territory that is unknown to the one he guides. That "territory" is the uncharted regions of divine truth in Scripture. Torrance summarizes the Spirit's activity as Guide. "The Spirit of Truth

101. Simpson, *The Epistles of Paul to the Ephesians and to the Colossians*, 38–39.

102. Hughes, *The Second Epistle to the Corinthians*, 134.

103. See Bromiley, "Interpretation of the Bible," 65; and Torrance, *God and Rationality*, 185.

104. Packer, "Infallible Scripture," 347.

105. Bloesch, "Sword of the Spirit," 72.

106. Torrance, *God and Rationality*, 185.

... directs us through the witness of the Holy Scripture, ... guiding us to know the Father in accordance with the way his revelation has taken in the Son."[107]

Yet another metaphor used to describe how the Holy Spirit brings understanding is the figure of one removing a covering from something hidden under a veil. This metaphor is suggested by the writer of 2 Cor 3:12–18. He says that a "veil" lies over the hearts of the sons of Israel; and, therefore, they cannot understand the reading of the old covenant. "But whenever a man turns to the Lord, the veil is taken away. Now the Lord is the Spirit; and where the Spirit of the Lord is, there is liberty." Keegan explains:

> The Jews, when they read Moses, read it with a veil over their eyes. Christians, however, can read Moses. Why? Because the veil has been removed by the Spirit that makes them able to read what the Spirit wants them to read in these books.[108]

The "unveiling" metaphor depicts the idea that the truth of Scripture is not clearly visible because it is shrouded in mystery. If the Spirit were not presently active revealing it, it "would remain buried."[109] He "unveils" this truth, making it visible as when one removes a covering from an object to expose it to the view of those who desire to see it. Therefore, he is called "the Spirit of Truth" because "truth is the unveiling of what was hidden, the manifestation of the divine Reality."[110]

MODELS

Besides these simple metaphors, a few more elaborate models are sometimes referred to in this discussion. Such models are not usually discussed extensively but rather are presented briefly in order to show, in an analogous way, how the Holy Spirit purveys understanding of Scripture. These include: the so called "Ghost in the Machine" or "*Deus ex Machina*" model;[111] the "Inspiration" model; and the "Teacher" model.

The "Ghost in the Machine" model depicts an extreme view in which the Holy Spirit mystically tells the reader the meaning of a text

107. Ibid., 192.

108. Keegan, *Interpreting the Bible*, 151.

109. Bloesch, "Sword of the Spirit," 72.

110. Torrance, *God and Rationality*, 167.

111. See Hirsch, "Current Issues," 302; and Grech, "The 'Testimonia' and Modern Hermeneutics," 324.

with little or no effort on the reader's part. "The Holy Spirit takes over the mind of the hearer and in some mysterious way enables or compels him to understand." The interpretation is suddenly provided independent of the reader.[112]

In effect, the *Deus ex Machina* renders hermeneutics irrelevant and unnecessary. Thus, scholars generally repudiate this view. Thiselton believes that those who discount or reject any role of the Holy Spirit in the hermeneutical process have something like the "Ghost in a Machine" model in mind. They reject the model and the notion of the Spirit's role along with it.[113] Scholars who do posit a role of the Spirit in hermeneutics also reject this model and look for some other way to describe the process.

Macquarrie admits that sometimes it may seem like "the understanding of the text just 'comes to' people without any conscious inquiry or effort to understand on their part." The understanding one gains may appear to have a gift-like character conferred by the Spirit apart from human endeavor. But this notion has the unacceptable tendency of drawing a sharp distinction between the God who addresses humanity and the Holy Spirit who enables his address to be understood. Macquarrie rejects the "Ghost in the Machine" model because in it "the Holy Spirit assumes the function of a mysterious *tertium quid*." In the activity of illumination the Spirit is not to be seen as an ambiguous third party mysteriously bestowing the interpretation of a passage.[114]

The "Ghost in the Machine" model thus often serves as a negative one in that it is usually used to depict how the Spirit *does not* function in interpretation. Agreeing with Macquarrie, Thiselton insists that the Holy Spirit plays a role in hermeneutics but not as a third party of ambiguous status over against both God and humanity. He writes:

> When the biblical writers or Christian theologians speak of the testimony of the Spirit, this is not to invoke some *additional* means of communicating the Word of God but is to claim that a message which is communicated in human language to human understanding addresses man *as* the Word of God.[115]

112. Macquarrie, *The Scope of Demythologizing*, 50.

113. Thiselton, *Two Horizons*, 85, 90, finds only "a minority of writers" who "sometimes invoke a doctrine of the Holy Spirit to argue that hermeneutics is unnecessary."

114. Macquarrie, *Scope of Demythologizing*, 36, 50.

115. Thiselton, *Two Horizons*, 90.

Prosper Grech likewise contends that if the activity of the Spirit is accurately recognized and properly admitted, his role will not be seen as one who intervenes suddenly to provide some contrived interpretation to difficult passages.[116] Roy B. Zuck, a strong advocate for recognizing the Holy Spirit's role, asserts: "To speak of the Spirit's part in hermeneutics is not to suggest some mysterious work that is beyond verification or validation." That is, he does not work in some mystical fashion in contradiction to common sense and logic.[117]

In comparison with the "Ghost in the Machine" model, the "Inspiration" model, at least at first glance, appears to be more fruitful in the positive direction. Inspiration naturally presents itself as a model of illumination because of the similarities of the two concepts. Both are held to be works of the Holy Spirit; both are related to God's attempt to communicate special revelation in Scripture; and both involve human instrumentality. Thus, while scholars seldom explicitly state that inspiration is a model for conceptualizing illumination, the notion is often implied in discussions of the latter.

Breck applies the "Inspiration" model, for example, in his "Reflections on the 'Hermeneutical Problem.'" He writes:

> We should recall that to the authors of the New Testament documents, Holy Scripture consisted of what we call the Old Testament. Their own writings, therefore, are in large measure interpretations of the Law, the Prophets and the other Writings of Israel. Once these apostolic works were themselves accepted as inspired "scripture" and acquired canonical status alongside the books of the Old Testament, successors to the apostles continued the activity of scriptural interpretation—not as a personal exercise undertaken on their own authority, but *under the continuing guidance of the Spirit within the ecclesial community.*[118]

Here the reader should note that Breck sees the Spirit's activity of giving understanding after the completion of the New Testament canon as being like his activity when these writings were being produced. Likewise, Peter Richardson implies that inspiration is a prototype of illumination in his discussion of Paul's distinction between Spirit and Letter. He sug-

---

116. Grech, "The 'Testimonia' and Modern Hermeneutics," 324.

117. Zuck, "The Role of the Holy Spirit," 126, 128.

118. Breck, "Exegesis and Interpretation," 90.

gests: "Paul's hermeneutic in 2 Cor. 3 can serve as a paradigm for our understanding of the hermeneutical task."[119]

Although the similarities between inspiration and illumination are apparent, the use of the former as a model for the latter is problematic for some scholars. Inspiration is itself an evasive concept. The insight to be gained by making one elusive notion a paradigm for envisioning another elusive notion is obviously limited. Also, while such an exercise in analogy does yield some benefit, many scholars are concerned about blurring the distinction between inspiration and illumination.

Though recognized to be similar and related, illumination and inspiration are considered to be two distinct functions of the Holy Spirit. True, illumination, like inspiration is "the preparation of heart and mind of man by the Holy Spirit to receive his revelation," as McDonald points out. Also, illumination, like inspiration involves "the quickening and heightening of man's apprehensive powers by the Spirit of God, whereby he is enabled to apprehend the Divine revelation and become an interpreter of it to his fellows." H. D. McDonald nevertheless contends:

> There is also a vast and vital difference between the illuminated Christian and the inspired prophet or apostle. In the former case the Holy Spirit works to give a vivid apprehension of truth already revealed: in the latter case there is a communication of truth altogether new.[120]

Rene Pache sees great danger in the confusion caused by relating illumination too closely to inspiration. She fears this "would soon lead to the same authority being given to man as belongs to the Word of God."[121] Likewise, Henry argues against the Barthian notion that illumination is simply a continuation of inspiration. He believes the Holy Spirit's original inspiration of chosen prophets and apostles in the production of Scripture must be distinguished from his ongoing illumination of readers of that Scripture. Henry wants to avoid the misunderstanding that results from overdrawing the similarities between the two concepts.[122] Inspiration, then, is limited in its usage as a prototype for conceptualizing how the Holy Spirit presently functions to bring understanding of Scripture.

---

119. Richardson, "Spirit and Letter: A Foundation for Hermeneutics," 214–18.

120. McDonald, *Theories of Revelation*, 234–36, 256.

121. Pache, *The Inspiration and Authority of Scripture*, 204.

122. Henry, *God Who Speaks and Shows*, 259–66.

The paradigm referred to most often is that of the Holy Spirit being a "Teacher." Statements about the Holy Spirit "teaching" believers the truths of Scripture, and readers "learning" as students under the "teaching ministry of the Spirit" are frequent.[123] Writers draw this idea from various biblical passages. In discussions of how readers come to understand the truths of Scripture, the statement attributed to Jesus himself in John 14:26 is often cited. "The Holy Spirit, whom the Father will send in My name, He will teach you all things." Another often cited passage is 1 John 2:27 where the writer says, "His anointing teaches you about all things." Ramm most succinctly states the model: "The true knowledge of God is gained with a teacher and a grammar, the Holy Spirit and the Sacred Writings." Ramm refers to the concept elsewhere in his writings, but he does not elaborate on the idea.[124]

Like Ramm, most other writers on the subject of illumination do not supply many particulars of how the "teacher" model portrays the Holy Spirit's role in the understanding of Scripture. Rather, they essentially only affirm the idea and then leave the model, with its implicit analogous features, to speak for itself. Presently, then, a detailed picture of how this paradigm conceptualizes the Spirit's function in hermeneutics cannot be drawn easily from the literature.

True, scholars usually do not elaborate on the idea of the Holy Spirit as a teacher. The frequent allusions to this paradigm and the intensity with which it is affirmed in the literature nevertheless show its importance. Besides those writers already referred to, a few other of the many possible examples are enough to make the point. Packer declares the Holy Spirit is "the church's only infallible teacher, to guide us into [Scripture's] meaning."[125] Bloesch recommends that since the key to the mystery of the text's meaning is divine illumination, "we must ask the Spirit to teach us the mystery."[126] F. E. Marsh insists that one requirement for understanding Scripture is "to be taught by him who inspired the Book." He states: "The Bible is a spiritual Book, to be understood by spiritual people, who are under the spiritual instruction of the Spiritual Teacher, the Holy Spirit."[127]

---

123. Zuck, "Role of the Holy Spirit," 121; Saucy, *The Bible: Breathed from God*, 111.

124. Ramm, *Witness of the Spirit*, 57, 64, 74.

125. Packer, "Contemporary Views of Revelation," 95.

126. Bloesch, "A Christological Hermeneutic," 100.

127. Marsh, *The Structural Principles of the Bible or How to Study the Word of God*,

For reasons already indicated in this discussion, the Holy Spirit as a "teacher" model may have considerable untapped potential. There seems to be a consensus among scholars concerning the veracity of the paradigm. Also, as stated above, although the idea is presented frequently, the particulars of the analogy are not extensively expounded in the literature. The epistemological overtones inherent in the "teaching/learning" dynamic do not seem to have been exhausted. How might the "teacher" model picture the Holy Spirit's epistemological relevance to Scripture? The next chapter explores the potential of this paradigm for visualizing the Holy Spirit's relationship to hermeneutics. Before that, however, other issues raised by positing a role of the Spirit in hermeneutics need to be considered.

Human Role in Interpretation

Thus far two issues pertaining to the Holy Spirit's role in hermeneutics have been discussed. These are: the issue of the *content and nature* of the illuminated message; and the issue of *how* the Holy Spirit acts to bring understanding of Scripture. Another issue is: "What is the *human role* when the Holy Spirit is involved in interpretation?" If the Holy Spirit "gives" the reader understanding, to what extent, if any, is the reader a vital participant in the endeavor? If the reader is a vital participant, what is the nature of his or her involvement; and how does it relate to the role of the Spirit?

COOPERATIVE PARTICIPATION

In a sense, part of the answer to one of the questions related to this issue has already been indicated in previous discussion. As noted above, serious scholars who posit a role of the Holy Spirit in interpretation reject the "Ghost in a Machine" model that essentially makes the reader only a passive recipient. Rather, they insist that the reader is a vitally active participant.

These scholars see the endeavor of interpretation as being a mutual effort of cooperation between the Spirit and the reader. W. W. Johnson writes:

> The work of the Spirit is uniquely associated with the effort of responsible hearing of the biblical text. We do not turn to ex-

---

277, 302.

egesis in isolation. Nor do we expect experiences of the Spirit in mystical ecstasy. Rather, we expect the work of the Spirit to be manifest in the specific task of seeking to hear the biblical word in its witness to Jesus Christ. The process of understanding the meaning of the biblical word for the present situation is a case both of serious industry and surprising insight.[128]

Zuck affirms the role of the Holy Spirit, but then he uses the work of inspiration to illustrate the cooperative nature of interpretation. "In the inspiration of the Bible the Holy Spirit was working but so were the human authors. In a similar way in the interpretation of the Bible, human work is involved"[129]

Understanding of Scripture is not an "either-or" exclusive enterprise—*either* by the Holy Spirit *or* by human endeavor. It is a "both-and" cooperative enterprise—*both* the Holy Spirit *and* the reader are active, vital participants. Breck asserts, "the exegete himself must participate in the process of divine revelation. He must submit himself and his skill to the guiding influence of the Holy Spirit if his efforts are to bear fruit." He adds: "Exegesis . . . is a *theandric* process, a divine-human enterprise based upon *synergy* or cooperation between the divine Spirit and the human interpreter."[130] Ramm says: "By the use of scientific philology *and* (my emphasis) the illumination of the Spirit we arrive at the clarity of Scripture." Thus, these scholars believe that those who are skilled in biblical studies and at the same time enlightened by the Spirit are the best interpreters. These interpreters are able to understand God's revelation in Scripture better than both those who are not so skilled and those who do not receive the Spirit's enlightenment.[131]

NORMAL LEARNING PROCESS

There is general agreement among scholars, then, that the Holy Spirit works in and through the native and acquired capabilities and tools of the interpreter—not independently of them. Illumination does not replace normal study; and, enlightenment by the Spirit does not ordinarily occur aside from the reader's diligent efforts. Thiselton agrees with Torrance that "the epistemological relevance of the Spirit does not mean

128. Johnson, "The Ethics of Preaching," 427.

129. Zuck, "Role of the Holy Spirit," 126.

130. Breck, "Exegesis and Interpretation," 91.

131. Ramm, *Protestant Biblical Interpretation*, 98.

that the problem of knowledge becomes Spirit-centered in the more obvious and superficial sense of the term." Thiselton insists that "the Holy Spirit works *through* human understanding."[132]

The notion that there is some inherent disparity between knowledge gained by normal study and understanding gained by the Spirit's illumination must then be rejected as invalid. Such a notion contradicts the position that interpretation is a cooperative enterprise involving both the Holy Spirit and the reader as active, vital participants. Thiselton accordingly argues against the implied Barthian position that the Holy Spirit's communication of revelation is somehow independent of all ordinary processes of human understanding. He says: "It in no way diminishes the crucial importance of the role of the Holy Spirit to say that the Spirit works *through* the normal processes of human understanding, and neither independently of them nor contrary to them."[133] Autry observes that "knowledge gained through 'natural' means is sometimes disparaged by those with an inadequate understanding of what it means to be 'spiritual.'" He notes that God is the Creator of humanity's mind and all the natural world known through the senses and reason. He suggests these "natural things" are "vehicles by which God makes his presence known." The question is not one of disparate elements but of the proper perspective or relationship with regard to "natural" understanding and "spiritual" understanding.[134]

Interpreters see no conflict between gaining understanding by normal reasoning abilities and receiving the enlightenment of the Holy Spirit. Thus, Nash is consistent when, on the one hand, he recognizes the dynamic of the Holy Spirit in interpretation; and on the other hand, he insists: "Any flight from reason and of logic is a flight from reality."[135] Torrance contends that "while [the Spirit] creates in us the ability to know God beyond all creaturely and human capacities this does not involve any suppression of our rational and critical powers." He adds: "In no way are we asked to take leave of our senses or to take irrational leaps."[136]

---

132. Thiselton, *Two Horizons*, 148–49.

133. Ibid., 146–47.

134. Autry, "Spiritual Man and Understanding," 18, 19. Also, see Dunnett, *The Interpretation of Holy Scripture*, 26.

135. Nash, *Word of God*, 41, 132.

136. Torrance, *God and Rationality*, 168.

Simply stated, then, illumination by the Holy Spirit comes in conjunction with normal human endeavor. Ordinary examination of materials, application of tools, and exercise of reason do not contradict pneumatic interpretation. Rather, diligent study and intellectual pursuit usually associated with learning processes are likewise appropriate and essential to the Holy Spirit's activity of enlightenment.

Hermeneutical Principles

In contending that normal learning processes are appropriate and essential to pneumatic interpretation, one is affirming that the fields of study normally associated with hermeneutical endeavors are valid and necessary. This affirmation that means the application of hermeneutical principles is compatible with and not contradictory to the Holy Spirit's illumination of Scripture. Fee states it simply: "The letter and the Spirit are not opposed to one another."[137] Accordingly, Fuller affirms: "The Holy Spirit does play an indispensable role in enabling the interpreter to gain the proper meaning of a biblical text." He also insists that the biblical interpreter "must expend just as much time and energy developing his exegetical skills and applying them to the hard work of understanding a text as others do who seek to determine the intended meanings of some group of ancient texts."[138]

Writers go even further in closely associating the application of hermeneutical principles with the Spirit's illumination of Scripture. Not only do they hold that the two are compatible and noncontradictory, they also hold that each activity is essential to the other in gaining a complete understanding of Scripture. Even when the Holy Spirit assists, ordinary hermeneutics is necessary. "Proper interpretation has to be in the Holy Spirit," Bromiley says. Yet, "normal hermeneutical procedures are not superseded. The general and technical principles still apply."[139] The full understanding of Scripture is a cooperative endeavor involving *both* the Holy Spirit and the reader as *vital* participants.

Illumination occurs in conjunction with, not in isolation from, normal application of hermeneutical principles. "The Holy Spirit may be said to work *through* human understanding, and not usually, if ever, through

---

137. Fee, "The Genre of New Testament Literature and Biblical Hermeneutics," 126.

138. Fuller, "Holy Spirit's Role in Biblical Interpretation," 190, 192.

139. Bromiley, "Interpretation of the Bible," 78.

processes which bypass the considerations discussed under the heading of hermeneutics."[140] In his article on the subject, Klooster strongly affirms the necessity of the Spirit's illumination. Yet he also notes: "Scripture is verbal and lingual: it is God's Word written. . . . Hence grammatical-literary exegesis is required in interpreting Scripture." He adds: "To understand Scripture every believer must read and interpret intelligently. The Holy Spirit does not produce revelational insight that 'automatically' provides the meaning of any passage." Klooster observes:

> A surprising thing occasionally happens. After one has left the laborious process of interpretation, . . . the meaning of the passage suddenly seems to jump to mind. . . . The interpreter's struggle to understand always precedes that unique experience; it does not occur in connection with a text on which one has expended no effort.[141]

Then, enlightenment by the Spirit and application of hermeneutics are complementary and mutually dependent factors in completing the interpretative process. Hermeneutics alone cannot take the reader beyond the cognitive level to grasp the "Supreme Truth" of Scripture; but that is not to say that hermeneutics is inappropriate or unnecessary. Ervin recognizes that "understanding of its [Scripture's] words is not possible apart from the agency of the Holy Spirit who first breathed them." He also cautions: "Inasmuch as biblical hermeneutics commits us to the task of translating and clarifying the sacred textual tradition, there can be no hermeneutical integrity apart from a critical, contextual exegesis."[142] Accordingly, Macquarrie is cautious about overextending the Spirit's place. "There is truth in the doctrine of the internal testimony of the Holy Spirit," he says; but "we cannot invoke it in order to relieve ourselves of investigating the problem of right interpretation of the Bible."[143]

The key is balance and recognizing that both normal hermeneutics and the Holy Spirit's illumination are necessary to complete understanding of Scripture. Berkely Mickelsen writes:

---

140. Thiselton, *Two Horizons*, 149.

141. Klooster, "Role of the Holy Spirit," 460–61, 470.

142. Ervin, "Hermeneutics," 13.

143. Macquarrie, *Scope of Demythologizing*, 37. Ebeling makes a similar point in *Theology and Proclamation*, 42.

> Some Christians fear that an emphasis upon such principles [of interpretation] ignores the illumination of the Holy Spirit. This fear has some foundation. Many have approached the Bible in a mechanical, rationalistic fashion. Fleeing from the extreme of mystical pietism, they have rushed into the error of regarding man's intellect as self-sufficient. . . . On the opposite side, there have been some sincere people who have thought that the witness of the Spirit in the heart of the believer enables him automatically to know the correct meaning. . . . True, the illumination of the Spirit is essential, but such illumination can be hindered by wrong approaches to the Scripture. The Christian must skillfully use sound principles in his efforts to uncover meaning.[144]

While "wrong approaches" can "hinder" illumination, proper hermeneutical endeavors promote enlightenment by the Holy Spirit, Klooster believes. "The biblical interpreter must read and study and struggle to understand the biblical text. The more self-consciously active the interpreter is in that process, the more likely is the Spirit's illumination."[145] Therefore, while the Spirit provides enlightenment, the role of the reader in interpretation is to engage in normal learning processes and employ usual hermeneutical principles and practices. Precisely in the activities of diligent study and consistent application of hermeneutics, the Holy Spirit faithfully functions in his role as an illuminator of Scripture.

RESPONSIVENESS

As important as participating in normal learning processes is, and as important as applying usual hermeneutical principles is, possibly the most significant role of the reader in understanding Scripture is *response*. This is a widely held view among scholars who address the issue of the Holy Spirit's illumination and the reader's role in interpretation. To know the full meaning of Scripture one must act on and appropriate the spiritual truths for his or her own life. The biblical message is not really understood, Klooster says, "unless one responds from the depths of the heart."[146]

In secular literary studies there is a recently developed system that makes the reader's response central to the understanding of literature. "Reader-response criticism," as it is called, emphasizes the reciprocal

144. Mickelsen, *Interpreting the Bible*, 4.

145. Klooster, "Role of the Holy Spirit," 460–61.

146. Ibid., 454.

relation between the text and the reader. The full meaning of literature is "created by" the reader in his or her response to the text.[147]

Many in the field of biblical studies cannot accept some of the premises of reader-response criticism. For example, reader-response critics contend that there is no purely objective content in a text apart from the meanings that are supplied by the reader's responses.[148] Many believe this emphasis on the subjective element to the exclusion of the objective element is untenable. This runs counter to the premise that such methods as the historical-critical method can indeed establish an element of objective content.

Scholars who posit a role of the Holy Spirit in hermeneutics usually reject such an overemphasis on the subjective element. They recognize the importance of the reader's response (including its subjective element); but they also contend for the objective element. For example, although he is not responding to "reader-response criticism" specifically, Henry addresses the basic issue of subjective-objective contents and the reader's response. He asserts that it is incorrect to make understanding of the Bible absolutely contingent upon the reader's response. Henry sees the validity and importance of both the subjective and objective elements in understanding. He writes:

> The revelational truth conveyed by objective scriptural disclosure itself stipulates the need for subjective illumination and appropriation. But to make the fact of illumination and need of appropriation a reason for compromising the perspicacity of scriptural teaching is unjustifiable.

In other words, the objective scriptural propositions "are plain enough for anyone to comprehend at face value."[149]

Although there is danger in overdrawing the subjective element, as stated above, scholars who posit a role of the Holy Spirit in hermeneutics generally also emphasize the necessity of the reader's response. One reason for this is, *responsiveness* is directly related to experience; and, as observed in an earlier section, scholars contend that knowledge of the "Supreme Truth" of Scripture is *experiential*. The one who truly understands and knows the truth of Scripture, knows by personally ex-

147. For a study of Reader-Response Criticism, the reader could begin with Tompkins, *Reader-Response Criticism*.

148. Keegan, *Interpreting the Bible*, 80–81.

149. Henry, *God Who Speaks and Shows*, 278–79.

periencing the reality of God revealed in Scripture. Thus, the goal of biblical interpretation is not just to give "an accurate description of biblical theology," Fuller declares. "Rather, the Holy Spirit's role is to change the heart of the interpreter." This occurs when the reader responds—when he or she "embraces" and "loves the message that is conveyed."[150]

On the negative side, lack of response or negative response results in failure to fully and properly understand—it results in incomplete or inaccurate interpretation. "The Holy Spirit in interpretation means . . . one who is not obeying the truth and is not yielding to the Lord, is unable to understand the Word fully," Zuck says.[151] This is why the unbeliever or the "natural" (*psychikos*) person, as Paul terms him (1 Cor 2), cannot understand (v. 14) God's wisdom hidden in a mystery (v. 7). Pinnock explains: "An unbeliever can comprehend the letter of Scripture, but is not inclined to commit himself to the appropriation of its truth for his life." An unbeliever is not inclined to respond.[152] "Thus, unbelievers do not *know* the full meaning of scriptural teaching, not because that meaning is unavailable to them in the words of the text, but because they refuse to act on and appropriate spiritual truths for their lives," Henry Virkler writes. They lack responsiveness.[153]

Autry and Fuller refer to Paul's discussion of the natural (*psychikos*) person in 1 Cor 2 to address the results of improper responsiveness. "The natural, *psychikos*, man may hear the gospel and 'understand' the words (in the ordinary sense)," but as long as his response is that of *psychikos* person, "it will remain for him foolishness and a stumbling block (I Cor. 1:22)," Autry explains. "The *psychikos* man, with his instinct for survival, must flee the cross." Therefore, "the *psychikos* man does not receive and cannot know these things [God's truths] because he wills otherwise."[154] A natural person's response is not conducive to receiving the enlightenment of the Holy Spirit. Fuller warns that "the deceitfulness of sin will cause even the most skilled exegete, by some legerdemain, to modify the meanings yielded up by the historical-grammatical data so they will not offend the ego." Failure to respond—failure to embrace the biblical

---

150. Fuller, "Holy Spirit's Role in Biblical Interpretation," 191–92, 194.

151. Zuck, "Role of the Holy Spirit," 125.

152. Pinnock, *Biblical Revelation*, 215.

153. Virkler, *Hermeneutics*, 30.

154. Autry, "The Spiritual Man and Understanding," 13–14, 22–23.

message—means one interprets it or understands it to be "foolishness" rather than "the power of God for salvation" (Rom 1:16).[155]

On the positive side, proper response to the Holy Spirit's enlightenment results in accurate interpretation and true understanding. The biblical message is really understood or, to use Klooster's words, "knowledge *of* God" is obtained and "heart-understanding" occurs when the reader "responds from the depths of the heart in love."[156] In contrast to the case of the *psychikos* ("natural") person, the *pneumatikos* ("spiritual") person can know the truths of God, "by his choice and the gracious aid of God's Spirit," Autry says. "Whenever and to whatever extent the *psychikos* man recognizes and accepts [responds to] the message . . . , at that point and to that degree he turns from being *psychikos* to being (or becoming) *pneumatikos*."[157] By responding, the reader turns from being unable to understand to being enlightened by the Holy Spirit.

If it is truly essential, then, the reader's role of responding introduces another aspect of the ever-present "hermeneutical circle." Illumination and the reader's response emphasizes submission to the content of the text. Thus, "the interpretation of the Bible takes on the circular form," Josef Bleicher notes. "In order to understand the text it is necessary to believe what the text expresses, which itself can only be known through understanding it."[158] Understanding—response/experience—understanding forms a circle that is completed only as a cooperative endeavor in which the Holy Spirit illuminates and the reader responds to understanding.

Who Can Be Co-Interpreters

With the human role in hermeneutics recognized, along with that of Spirit's, the issue which remains is the question: "*Who* can be co-interpreters with the Holy Spirit?" Are only select individuals or groups of persons capable of receiving the Spirit's illumination of Scripture? Or,

155. Fuller, "Holy Spirit's Role in Biblical Interpretation," 191–92, 198.

156. Klooster, "Role of the Holy Spirit," 454–55, 463. Gadamer, in *Truth and Method*, 297, emphasizes the reader's response without distinguishing between the negative and positive. He says: "The word of scripture addresses us, and . . . only the person who allows himself to be addressed—whether he believes or whether he doubts—understands."

157. Autry, "The Spiritual Man and Understanding," 14, 23.

158. Bleicher, *Contemporary Hermeneutics*, 105. Krentz also notes this aspect of the "hermeneutical circle" in *Historical-Critical Method*, 70.

are all believers potential recipients of enlightenment? To what extent can non-believers understand the Supreme Truths of Scripture? Are non-believers also potential recipients of enlightenment?

BELIEVERS

Among both contemporary Catholic and Protestant writers, the basic answer to these questions is that all persons are potential recipients of the Holy Spirit's illumination. Thus, all persons are potential participants in the cooperative endeavor of pneumatic interpretation of Scripture. Klooster rhetorically asks: "Do biblical commentators possess a special gift of the Spirit for interpretation and does illumination occur uniquely in such interpreters?" Like others who posit a role of the Spirit in hermeneutics, his answer is, "No." He says: "The illumination of the Holy Spirit operates in the lives of all believers."[159] Logically, "the person who has a share in the faith (of the church) . . . also has a share in the Spirit, and is therefore qualified for interpretation of the Bible in its fullness of the Spirit."[160]

The church does recognize those who are especially qualified in understanding the Bible. These are often delegated the special responsibility of interpreting and communicating its truths. Johnson notes that certain persons are set aside for the task of "hearing" the Scripture's message. "Because of the obvious demands of time and effort and the clear distribution of gifts . . ., it is apparent that not all members . . . can pursue extensively the issues of hearing." He adds: "This does not [however] cut off the individual Christian from his own reading of the Bible."[161] Klooster refers to the special offices in Eph 4 and says: "Those gifted and appointed to these offices are specially qualified by the Spirit of the ascended Christ; the interpretation of Scripture is a significant responsibility of such persons." He also notes: "The Spirit's illumination is no more guaranteed the professional exegete than the ordinary believer."[162]

Special qualifications and specific delegation to the task of interpretation do not then reserve illumination for a select few. Henry observes:

> Significantly, the New Testament does not specify that true exposition of Scripture is a special gift of the Spirit reserved for only a

159. Klooster, "Role of the Holy Spirit," 452, 459.

160. Stuhlmacher, "Theological Interpretation of Holy Scripture," 6.

161. Johnson, "The Ethics of Preaching," 425.

162. Klooster, "Role of the Holy Spirit," 468–69.

few specially endowed Christians, a chosen illuminati, whether a cadre of scholars, or ecclesiastics, or charismatics.

Rather, "the Bible was—and is still—addressed to the multitudes, to masses of the poor, uneducated and even enslaved." Spirit-illumination assures that these persons may understand the message of Scripture.[163] Enlightenment by the Holy Spirit, Pache says, means "the essentials of Scripture can be apprehended by any spiritual man, even though, humanly speaking, he possesses only a modest education."[164]

The view that Spirit-enlightenment and understanding of Scripture is available and open to all readers is contrary to the older Roman Catholic position. Walter Kasper concisely states the former position: "Authentic interpretation can of course be carried out only by the teaching ministry of the church endowed with a special charisma, i.e., the totality of the episcopate together with the Pope." In other words, illumination and enlightened interpretation are the preserve of the church hierarchy.[165] Anthony Palma calls this "the traditional view" in which "the individual believer is denied access to the Holy Spirit as the interpreter of the Word."[166]

The Reformation reacted against this and other positions of the Roman Catholic Church. The Reformers rejected the "chosen illuminati" notion, "rightly insisting that the Spirit is bound by no human institution."[167] The conviction that every member of the "priesthood of believers" receives Spirit-illumination followed from other basic Reformation principles. "The priesthood of all believers was at the heart of the Reformation," Klooster notes. Thus, since then interpretation of Scripture in Protestant circles has been the privilege and responsibility of the entire believing community. That task is not restricted to a priesthood of illuminati.[168]

Especially since Vatican II, Roman Catholic writers have also affirmed the privilege and responsibility of all believers to read and understand Scripture. Among the principles of this Council was "the insistence

---

163. Henry, *God Who Speaks and Shows*, 280–83.

164. Pache, *Inspiration and Authority of Scripture*, 202.

165. Kasper, "Roman Catholic Theology," 510.

166. Palma, *The Spirit—God in Action*, 110.

167. Breck, "Exegesis and Interpretation," 80.

168. Klooster, "Role of the Holy Spirit," 452.

that all persons be given full and easy access to Scripture."[169] Now Roman Catholic scholars, like Schneiders, write concerning divine assistance in interpretation and ordinary Christians being able to gain correct interpretation.[170] Harrington is one of several Roman Catholic contributors to a biblical studies series designed to help all Christians better understand Scripture. He writes *Interpreting the New Testament: A Practical Guide* as "a beginner's book" to help readers in gaining "spiritual insight from the New Testament."[171] Another Catholic scholar, Keegan, writes "a popular introduction to biblical hermeneutics" in which he especially relates the activity of the Holy Spirit to interpretation.[172] Catholics now tend to see illumination as operating among all believers.

NON-BELIEVERS

The question of the non-believer participating in the Spirit's ministry of illumination and understanding the Supreme Truths of Scripture is more difficult. On the one hand, there is a sense, scholars say, in which the unbeliever cannot understand spiritual truth. Yet, on the other hand, the non-believer does seem to understand Scripture, including spiritual truth, and even becomes converted.

Certainly, the unbeliever who has hermeneutical skills, like the believer, can cognitively comprehend what the writers are saying. Concerning the work of agnostics and atheists, Fuller contends: "To the extent that they are skilled in exegesis, their exposition of what the biblical writers intended to say will be accurate."[173]

The question is: Does Spirit-illumination of Scripture occur in the case of the non-believer, taking him or her beyond the cognitive level to the "spiritual" level of understanding. Many writers believe that it does. Otherwise how could conversion ever occur? Regeneration cannot be made a prerequisite to illumination since enlightened understanding is necessary to believing and accepting the gospel.[174] Schneiders notes that even "people who do not stand explicitly within the Judeo-Christian

169. McIntire, "Vatican Council II," 1136.

170. Schneiders, "Faith, Hermeneutics, and the Literal Sense," 729, 733–34.

171. Harrington, *Interpreting the New Testament*, vii–xi, 126.

172. Keegan, *Interpreting the Bible*, 151, 155, 161, 163.

173. Fuller, "Holy Spirit's Role in Biblical Interpretation," 192, 197.

174. See Autry, "The Five Dimensions of Hermeneutics," 17–19; and Fuller, "Holy Spirit's Role in Biblical Interpretation," 191–92.

tradition have understood the biblical text sufficiently to be genuinely moved by it, even to the point of becoming Christians."[175]

The distinction to be made is not between "believers" and "non-believers" in the sense of "converted" and "unconverted." The correct distinction is between "believers" and "unbelievers" in the sense of "spiritual" (*pneumatikos*) and "natural" (*psychikos*). As seen above, it is "natural" person who does not receive enlightenment because of a negative response to what he does understand. Even "natural" people can receive enlightenment, however, if and when he responds positively to the message of Scripture. "Whenever and to whatever extent the *psychikos* man recognizes and accepts the message of the cross, at that point and to that degree he turns from being *psychikos* to being (or becoming) *pneumatikos*."[176] Thus, while in an unconverted state, the non-believer can even then receive Holy Spirit illumination and turn from being *psychikos* to being *pneumatikos* at least to the extent of being enlightened concerning personal redemption. The unbeliever who chooses to remain *psychikos* is the only kind of person who cannot be a cooperative participant in the Holy Spirit's ministry of Scripture illumination.

Summary

Several important and difficult issues are raised when a role of the Spirit in hermeneutics is posited. The most significant of these are covered in the consideration of the following questions: What is the contents and nature of the Spirit-illuminated message? How does the Holy Spirit illuminate Scripture? What is the human role in interpretation when the Spirit assists? Who can be co-interpreters with the Holy Spirit? Scholars generally have difficulty conceptualizing such mysterious, intangible phenomena. Writers do, though, make some attempt to articulate answers to these questions.

Regarding the *content and nature* of the Spirit-illuminated message, writers suggest that the Holy Spirit enables readers to gain an understanding of Scripture's Supreme Truth that is beyond humanity's normal cognitive level of understanding. Also, what the reader is enabled to comprehend may be beyond what the writer understood; but this does not include "new revelations" nor strictly "private interpreta-

175. Schneiders, "Faith, Hermeneutics, and the Literal Sense," 734.
176. Autry, "The Spiritual Man and Understanding," 14.

tions." That is, in illumination the Holy Spirit does not give previously unknown cognitive information nor original special revelation beyond that already contained in Scripture. The right of private understanding does not include the right of individualistic, private interpretation. Interpretation is community oriented, and correct Scripture understanding has a communal character. Finally, scholars suggest that Holy Spirit illuminated understanding and knowledge of Scripture is experiential. The supreme knowledge gained by enlightenment is experiential knowledge of Jesus Christ—God's ultimate revelation to humanity and the essence of Scripture's message.

Writers use various metaphors and models to conceptualize and articulate *how* the Spirit brings about understanding of Scripture. The metaphors include picturing the Holy Spirit as one who "shines light" on the Truth ("illuminates" the Truth), "guides" into all Truth, and "unveils" the Truth. These metaphorical comparisons are both stated and implied in the literature. The models used by scholars include the "Ghost in the Machine" or "*Deus ex Machina*" model, the "Inspiration" model, and the "Teacher" model. The "Ghost in the Machine" model envisions the Holy Spirit as being some kind of spook that mystically tells the reader the meaning of a text with little or no effort on the reader's part. This is a negative or counter model in that it is used by writers to tell how the Holy Spirit does not function in illumination. The "Inspiration" model likens the Spirit's activity in illumination to that in inspiration. Though it is considered to be a beneficial paradigm, many scholars are cautions about its usage because it tends to blur the distinction between two separate functions of the Holy Spirit. The "Teacher" model delineates illumination by portraying the Spirit and the reader in a teacher-pupil dynamic. This model is the one most often referred to by writers and is therefore presently the most fruitful paradigm for conceptualizing the Holy Spirit's relationship to hermeneutics.

Those who posit a role of the Holy Spirit in hermeneutics also insist that the *human role* is essential and genuine. Interpretation is seen as being a cooperative enterprise in which both the Spirit and the reader are vitally active participants. Therefore, the human endeavors of normal study and application of hermeneutical principle are valid and necessary. Illumination occurs in conjunction with, not in isolation from, these human efforts. Also, the responsiveness of the reader is significant. The interpreter can participate in illumination and receive enlightened understanding of Scripture only when responding positively to the Holy Spirit's message.

All persons are potential *co-interpreters* with the Holy Spirit. Interpretation of Scripture is not the exclusive privilege of a chosen illuminati. Both believers and non-believers can experience enlightenment in positive responsiveness to the Spirit's activity of illumination. Both Protestant and Roman Catholic scholars now affirm the view that illumination means correct interpretation of Scripture is available to all receptive readers.

CONCLUSION

The issue of the Holy Spirit's relationship to interpretation in contemporary biblical hermeneutics has to do with two basic concerns. The initial concern is: Does the Holy Spirit have an authentic, definitive role in the hermeneutical process? The subsequent concern is: What major questions are raised when the Spirit is envisioned to have a role in interpretation and how can these questions be answered? The present study allows for several observations concerning this issue and its related questions.

One of these observations is that there is a limited amount of material in current literature on the issue of the Holy Spirit's relationship to hermeneutics. The Spirit's function in interpretation is an intangible component. Many writers do not discuss the subject or they only refer to it briefly in passing. Other writers do address the issue and its related questions, but they do so with only limited discussion. Presently, material in the literature provides a beginning, but only a beginning, delineation of the Holy Spirit's role in hermeneutics.

A second observation is, writers who address the issue of the Holy Spirit's relationship to hermeneutics appear to be divided on the question of whether he plays a vital role in interpretation. On the one hand, there are some who seem to deny or at least greatly limit the Spirit's role in interpretation. On the other hand, there are many who clearly and assuredly affirm that his role is genuine and essential. In fact, most scholars who consider the Bible to be God's special revelation to humanity do envision a role of the Holy Spirit in hermeneutics.

A third observation is that scholars who envision a role of the Holy Spirit in hermeneutics have considerable difficulty fully and clearly addressing the questions raised by this position. Exactly how the Spirit functions in this role; how he and the reader interrelate in the process;

and the results of the Holy Spirit's activity in interpretation, are arduous ideas to conceptualize. A problem with semantics contributes to the difficulty. Writers generally lack specificity in their usage of important terminology. Broad and varied use of certain terms leaves the reader uncertain about the scholars' views concerning the Holy Spirit's involvement. If the Spirit plays a role in the hermeneutical process, does he play a role in all phases or only part of them? In which aspects of understanding Scripture does the Spirit have a role and in which aspects does he not have a role? What is the functional relationship between the Holy Spirit and the human interpreter in understanding Scripture? These and other questions are open to more comprehensive delineation and discussion. The next chapter pursues this task by suggesting and using clearly defined terms, and by considering methodology for describing the Holy Spirit's relationship to the hermeneutical process.

4

Methodology: A Proposed Model

INTRODUCTION

THIS STUDY OF CONTEMPORARY hermeneutics reveals a limited discussion of the Holy Spirit's relationship to the process. Some scholars do not discuss the topic. Others either deny that the Spirit has a role in this enterprise or they greatly limit his participation. Even those who affirm the Holy Spirit's role in hermeneutics usually do not discuss the idea in extensive detail. There is a need for further discussion of the issues related to the idea that the Holy Spirit is involved in the hermeneutical process.

As proposed in chapter 1 above, recognizing and using paradigms or models becomes especially helpful. What is needed is a model or some models that can be used in an analogous way. Such a model or models could possibly allow theologians more distinctly to envision and more extensively to describe the role of the Holy Spirit and the results of his involvement in understanding Scripture. Avery Dulles points out: "Theological models are for religion, in an analogous way, what theoretical models are for science."[1] They allow theologians to imagine and articulate the mysteries of God and his activities. Ian Ramsey lists three ways in which models help theologians to be imaginative and articulate in situations such as the present consideration. One, models are "builders of discourse, . . . giving rise to large-scale interpretation of phenomena that so far lack a theological mapping." Two, models "enable us to make

---

1. Dulles, *Models of Revelation*, 32.

sense of discourse whose logical structure is so perplexing as to inhibit literacy." And three, models "enable us to talk of what eludes us."[2]

Can one find or imagine a model or some models that might provide additional details about the Spirit's function in hermeneutics? Is there a model or are there models that can supply more comprehensive answers to critical questions raised by positing a role of the Holy Spirit in understanding Scripture? Hopefully, such a model or models would arise and present itself or themselves spontaneously. Ramsey notes that for theological models to be reliable and useful, they "must chime in with the phenomena; they must arise in a moment of insight or disclosure."[3] Is there such a model or are there such models for envisioning the Holy Spirit's relationship to understanding Scripture? In chapter 3 above, discussion of the present positions among scholars reveals that in fact one especially promising model does arise in the current contemplation of the topic at hand. That model is the "teacher" model.

What is meant by a "teacher" model is a model in which the illumination and understanding of Scripture is seen to be a process analogous to the teaching and learning process. In this model the Spirit is pictured as performing a function in the hermeneutical process similar to the function performed by a teacher in the learning process. The Scripture reader, or expositor, is pictured as having a role similar to that of the student. Also, in the "teacher" model the outcomes of the teaching/learning process are said to picture the results of illumination/exposition.

The idea of the Holy Spirit being a teacher is as old as the Scriptures themselves. The writer in Neh 9:20 suggests that God gave his Spirit "to instruct" the Israelites in the wilderness. In 1 Cor 2:11, Paul draws an analogy. The spirit of a human being knows the thoughts of that person as no other person can know them. Likewise, no one knows the thoughts of God like the Spirit of God. In the mind of Paul this evidently makes the Holy Spirit the best *teacher* of the things of God. Thus he claims authority for the things that he had previously spoken to his readers because he had been "taught by the Spirit" (v. 13). John 14:26 records a promise said to have been given by Jesus to his followers: "The Holy Spirit, whom the Father will send in My name, He will teach you all things." Admittedly, these passages do not explicitly relate the Spirit's

---

2. Ramsey, *Models and Mysteries*, 14–15.

3. Ibid., 15.

teaching ministry to Scripture; but the main point is that they picture him in the "teacher" role.

One can easily see why Christian writers from Origen to the present have used the teacher model to speak of how the Holy Spirit brings understanding of God's special message to humanity. William Abraham considers "a good teacher inspiring his students" to be a familiar, insightful paradigm for discussing how God inspired the writers of Scripture. He notes: "The divine inspiration of the Bible has traditionally been associated with instruction and teaching."[4] Chapter 3 above shows the importance of the teacher model in a contemporary discussion of illumination.

The Scripture authors, and the early Christian writers who followed their lead, saw that the activities of a teacher gave insights—in an analogous way—into the activity of God in communicating special revelation. Contemporary writers continue to utilize the analogy because they believe it has the ability to picture God's ongoing operation of giving understanding. To use Ramsey's words again, these writers believe the teacher model "enables us to talk of what eludes us" regarding the activity of the Holy Spirit relative to understanding Scripture.[5]

As noted in the previous chapter, the teacher model is the one most often referred to in the literature. Unlike the "ghost-in-the-machine" and the "inspiration" paradigms, the teacher model enjoys a wide consensus among scholars concerning its veracity and usefulness. No other model presents itself with such force as a logical paradigm for picturing the Holy Spirit's relationship to hermeneutics. This chapter adopts the idea that the teacher model is the best available model for "theological mapping" of the Holy Spirit's relationship to hermeneutics. Advocated here is the proposal that this model has the potential to allow theologians to envision that relationship and its consequences more distinctively and extensively.

In any exercise of "theological mapping" using models, care must be taken on two sides. On the one hand, care must be taken not to "stretch" the model too far so as to avoid illogical absurdity. For example, Janet Martin Soskice notes: "Christian presuppositions make it absurd to extend the model of God's fatherhood so far as to say that he has a wife." On the other hand, a certain freedom must be taken to "stretch" the model to the point that its full projective capacities are realized. For example,

---

4. Abraham, *The Divine Inspiration of Holy Scripture*, 63–65.

5. Ramsey, *Models and Mysteries*, 14–15.

the same fatherhood model is appropriately "stretched" to picture "the 'heavenly father' to be perfect in love and knowledge" even though the love and the knowledge of earthly fathers are not so perfect.[6]

While absurd conclusions are to be avoided, the very purpose of analogous models is to extend understanding from that which is known to that which is unknown. Further, models are intended to extend conceptualization from that which is concrete to that which is abstract. Morris L. Bigge explains: "*Models*, in essence, *are expectancies.*" They "enable persons to predict, interpolate, and extrapolate further knowledge." One who productively applies a model moves beyond what is given to new understandings "by matching what is presently experienced to an acquired model and reading much from the model."[7] Thus, the present study proposes that the endeavor of teaching can be "stretched" to allow one to imagine how and what God seeks to communicate to humanity through Scripture.

Before considering this model, the difficulty with semantics, observed in the conclusion of chapter 3, must be addressed. For clarity of communication, the definitions and use of certain terms must be more specific and more precise. In subsequent discussion, the term "meaning," when it is used in reference to Scripture, refers to the message that the author conveyed to the readers in the original historical situation. The term "significance" refers to the theologically consequential message God intended or intends to be conveyed to readers. The "original significance" refers to the theologically consequential message that God intended to be conveyed to the readers in the original historical situation. The "contemporary significance" refers to the theologically consequential message that God intends for modern readers. The term "interpretation" includes the "meaning" and the "original significance" as defined here. "Exegesis" is the attempt to discover the "interpretation" of a text. "Exposition" is the activity or the results of giving an explanation of the "interpretation" and setting forth the "contemporary significance" of a passage. An "expositor," then, is an "interpreter" of the original intent of a text as well as an "expounder" of its contemporary significance. Also, the term "reader" has special meaning in this discussion. The "reader" is one who seeks both to "interpret" Scripture and to understand its "significance." The phrase "understanding of Scripture" includes all of that

6. Soskice, *Metaphor and Religious Language*, 64, 116.

7. Bigge, *Learning Theories for Teachers*, 249–50.

which is understood in "interpretation" and "exposition" of Scripture. The term "illumination" refers to the activity of the Holy Spirit in assisting contemporary readers to understand Scripture.

With these terms clarified, this chapter looks at what happens in the common teacher/student learning process, draws some analogies along the way, and indicates a Spirit/reader paradigm for understanding illumination. The plan is to analyze some paradigms of teaching and learning in the common world of human agents. Then, with insights from these paradigms, it is proposed that extrapolations can be made, allowing one to envision the nature and result of the Holy Spirit's relationship to hermeneutics.

There are numerous kinds of teaching styles, but writers in education often group them into a few basic types according to certain shared characteristics of teaching approaches. The present discussion is benefited by analyzing three basic types and the three teaching paradigms commonly associated with them. These three basic paradigms are common to the literature and are identified by various terms. For the present discussion the following terminology is adopted: one, the term "authoritarian" identifies the paradigm in which the teacher, in an autocratic manner, dispenses knowledge and understanding to the student; two, the term "laissez-faire" identifies the paradigm in which the teacher deliberately gives only minimal direction and assistance; and, three, the term "facilitator" identifies the paradigm in which the teacher is proactive along with the student in a mutually participatory endeavor.

The following analyses and descriptions are admittedly simplified for the sake of clarity. They omit the many amplifications and variations in order to picture easily understood paradigms which can serve as basic reference models. This simplification also includes a deliberate attempt to show and emphasize each paradigm's distinctiveness. By purposeful design their distinguishing characteristics and features become clearer as the discussion progresses.

One must be aware that such simplification includes the possible danger that part of the picture may be omitted. Notwithstanding this potential danger, the great advantage here is that it provides readily grasped holistic paradigms from which extrapolations can be made for envisioning the Holy Spirit's relationship to hermeneutics. This project is most successful when the paradigms are sharply delineated, with their differences clearly evident, so that comparisons and contrasts can be made easily.

Using a tripartite outline, the following analysis and synthesis has a three-point focus: one, the leading agent (teacher/Holy Spirit); two, the receiving agent (student/reader); and, three, the outcomes or results (learning/understanding). The three basic teaching/learning paradigms are analyzed in order to see how they possibly picture the phenomenon of understanding Scripture. First, the role of the teacher is considered. Observations are made concerning how the role of the teacher in each paradigm possibly pictures the role of the Spirit in illuminating Scripture. Second, the role of the student is considered. Observations are made concerning how the role of the student in each paradigm possible pictures the role of the reader in understanding of Scripture. Third, the outcomes of the teaching/learning process are considered. Observations are made concerning how the outcomes in each paradigm possibly picture the results in illumination and exposition.

Before continuing, two preliminary qualifications to the discussion need to be noted. One, this study is not primarily an examination of epistemology and learning in general. The writer makes no claim that the study is exhaustive with regard to epistemological theory or learning theory. Rather, as stated above, the researcher intends simply to look at basic paradigms of teaching/learning in the common world of human agents and draw some obvious analogies for envisioning the Holy Spirit's relationship to hermeneutics. Two, the intent is not, so to speak, to "wrench" the teaching/learning paradigms in order to draw out every possible legitimate comparison. Rather, the intent is simply to look for the analogous points that spontaneously arise and, then, to suggest how these give insights into illumination and exposition.

ROLE OF THE LEADING AGENTS

With these preliminary qualifications in mind, the first step in the proposed analysis and synthesis is to look at the teacher's and the Holy Spirit's roles. In both secular education literature and religious education literature the teacher's role is viewed to be different in each of the three basic teaching/learning paradigms. The very terms "authoritarian," "laissez-faire," and "facilitator" indicate and emphasize the distinctiveness of the teacher's role in the paradigms.[8] These three paradigms are looked at in order to see the

---

8. This terminology reflects the perceived role of the teacher, rather than that of the student. The present discussion, in all of its sections, follows the lead of the literature in using these terms.

nature of the teacher's involvement in each one. What might the teacher's role, as seen in these paradigms, imply concerning the nature and diversity of the Holy Spirit's role in the hermeneutical process?

Authoritarian Paradigm

ROLE OF THE TEACHER

The first paradigm under consideration is the authoritarian paradigm. In this paradigm emphasis is upon the fact that the teacher is the authority who possesses a body of knowledge which he or she delivers to the student. "The teacher's role is to pass on knowledge of reality and to be an example of the ethical ideal."[9] The teacher knows what the student needs to know, think and do. B. F. Skinner's behavioralism method of teaching and learning follows this approach. He is one of the leading proponents of this method.[10]

The authoritarian teacher, Bigge says, "regards himself as the sole active agent and considers students passive receivers of instructions and information."[11] In this paradigm, "the teacher functions as manager where teaching is considered as a pipeline. The role of teacher as manager is to manage the flow of information through this line."[12] The learning process consists of a "more or less mechanical acquisition of knowledge, facts, and skills." In the extreme form of this paradigm "the teacher is something of an oral textbook. He needs only to be audible, understandable, and—hopefully—encyclopedic."[13]

Various terms are used to identify this paradigm and to describe the teacher's role in it. The authors of *Methods for Teaching: A Skills Approach* identify it as "expository teaching." The role of the teacher is that of an information giver who has "knowledge and whose job it is to pass this knowledge directly on to students."[14] Gary D. Fenstermacher and Jonas F. Soltis term the approach of this paradigm the "executive approach" in which the teacher is viewed as "a person charged with

9. Knight, *Philosophy and Education*, 49.

10. For the particulars of Skinner's views and practices, see Skinner, *The Technology of Teaching*.

11. Bigge, *Learning Theories for Teachers*, 324.

12. Sergiovanni and Starratt, *Supervision: Human Perspectives*, 338.

13. Melby, *The Teacher and Learning*, 76.

14. Jacobsen et al, *Methods for Teaching: A Skills Approach*, 145.

bringing about certain learnings."[15] John P. Miller and Wayne Seller call it the "Transmission Position." "Teachers in this position tend to play a directive role in the learning process. Instruction in this position is often didactic."[16] Gilbert A. Peterson uses two terms to describe the role of the teacher in the authoritarian paradigm: "manipulator" and "inculcator." The teacher closely manages the learning process to insure that the student learns certain facts, concepts, skills and attitudes.[17]

ROLE OF THE HOLY SPIRIT

In this paradigm the Holy Spirit's role in illumination would be much like that in the Ghost-in-a-Machine model discussed above in chapter 3. As the all-knowing One he would simply give the Bible reader the meaning and significance with little effort on the reader's part. The Holy Spirit would transmit previously unknown information and understanding in a rather mechanical way directly to the reader. This might include not only the original significance and the contemporary significance but also the author's original meaning.

In revealing the original significance and/or the contemporary significance, the Holy Spirit would be much like the teacher who takes a textbook and, with the student following along, highlights certain important parts. The purpose is not only to pass along information but also to emphasize the relevance and significance of the contents. Here the role of the Holy Spirit would be to make the reader keenly aware of the theologically consequential message that God intends to be conveyed by the text.

Laissez-faire Paradigm

ROLE OF THE TEACHER

A second basic approach to teaching is described by the "laissez-faire" paradigm. Whereas in the authoritarian paradigm the teacher's role is direct and proactive, in the laissez-faire paradigm the teacher's role is the opposite extreme. He or she is indirect and much less active. The laissez-faire teacher "deliberately abstains from student direction, . . . he

---

15. Fenstermacher and Soltis, *Approaches to Teaching*, 4.

16. Miller and Seller, *Curriculum: Perspectives and Practices*, 56.

17. Peterson, "The Christian Teacher," 86.

does not really lead at all."[18] Rather than being an authoritarian director, he or she is a minimally active "adviser."[19] Carl R. Rogers is a leading proponent of the nondirective method of teaching.[20]

As in the case of the authoritarian type, writers use various terms to identify the laissez-faire paradigm and to describe the teacher's role in it. In *Methods for Teaching* it is characterized as student oriented "discovery" learning.[21] Peterson describes the laissez-faire teacher as a "motivator" whose primary function is to inspire students. The teacher's emphasis is on creating a certain learning atmosphere rather than on communicating content.[22] Fenstermacher and Soltis call this the "therapist" approach. The teacher is viewed as "an empathetic person charged with helping individuals grow personally and reach a high level of self-actualization, understanding, and acceptance."[23] With a similar emphasis, Miller and Seller identify this as the "transformation" position. Central to this paradigm is the view that the student is able to carry out his or her own learning. The main task of the teacher, then, is simply to develop a trusting climate.[24]

ROLE OF THE HOLY SPIRIT

In a laissez-faire paradigm the role of the Holy Spirit in hermeneutics would be quite limited. His role in giving understanding of Scripture would be no more than it would be in giving understanding of any other written material. In that God is the sustainer of the universe and the supplier of all its energies, in a general sense the Holy Spirit may be seen as an enabler in all human activities. Thus, in a general sense the Holy Spirit could be said to be present and—in an indirect, laissez-faire fashion—to "enable" the believer to understand Scripture just as he "enables" the English student to understand Shakespeare. This limited role of the Holy Spirit, as pictured in the laissez-faire paradigm, describes the view of Walter Kaiser and James Lee discussed in chapter 3 above.

18. Bigge, *Learning Theories*, 324.

19. See Knight, *Philosophy and Education*, 94.

20. For the particulars of Rogers' views and practices the reader should see Rogers, *Freedom to Learn*.

21. Jacobsen et al, *Methods for Teaching*, 143.

22. Peterson, "The Christian Teacher," 86.

23. Fenstermacher and Soltis, *Approaches to Teaching*, 4.

24. Miller and Seller, *Curriculum*, 148.

Beyond this general "enabler" role, the Spirit's function in a laissez-faire paradigm would be to confirm the truth of Scripture and convince the reader of its authority. He would be much like the teacher who is present to encourage the learner and confirm the relevance and worth of the student's *independent* discoveries. This would correspond to Berkouwer's view as seen in chapter 3 above. Berkouwer denies or at least limits the present role of the Holy Spirit in the activity of understanding Scripture. However, he does attribute to him the specific function of convincing the reader of the text's authoritative nature. In a laissez-faire type of role, then, the Holy Spirit would simply be present to create an atmosphere of faith and conviction regarding the text. It would not include giving the Scripture reader any extraordinary assistance in understanding the text.

Facilitator Paradigm

ROLE OF THE TEACHER

A third basic type of teaching is described in the facilitator paradigm. "The teacher working from this position attempts to facilitate the development of student inquiry skills." The teacher also attempts "to stimulate inquiry with questions and probes."[25] In this paradigm, "teaching is conceived as a mediating process within which, students with the help of teachers, interact with information and ideas in terms of personal meanings and previous learnings."[26] In the spectrum from direct and proactive involvement to indirect and nonactive involvement, the teacher's role in this paradigm is midway between that of the authoritarian teacher and the laissez-faire teacher. One should especially note that the teacher in this paradigm is a "facilitator" not just because he or she makes learning easier or more simplified; the teacher is a "facilitator" in that he or she actively assists and aids the student in the learning process.[27]

---

25. Miller and Seller, *Curriculum*, 111.

26. Sergiovanni and Starratt, *Supervision*, 341.

27. The present writer is aware of the fact that Carl Rogers uses the term "facilitator" to describe the teacher in his non-directive method that fits what is herein called the laissez-faire paradigm. Rogers' seems to mean that the teacher's proper role is simply to make learning possible in an unassertive fashion. In contrast, in the third basic paradigm presently being discussed the teacher is a "facilitator" who not only makes learning possible but also actively helps the student.

As in the case of both the authoritarian and the laissez-faire types, writers use various terms to speak of the facilitator paradigm and to describe the teacher's role in it. Miller and Seller call it the "transaction" position in which "both the teacher and the child share control of learning tasks."[28] With this paradigm in view, T. W. Moore describes learning as "a co-operative enterprise in which the pupil is encouraged to take the initiative, . . . the teacher providing the help needed to ensure that the child gets the necessary intellectual stimulation and opportunities for development."[29] Bigge characterizes the teacher in the facilitator paradigm as "a democratic teacher" who leads students in study and encourages them to think for themselves.[30] Peterson notes that a "facilitator" teacher employs various aids and techniques to enhance the learning experience.[31]

ROLE OF THE HOLY SPIRIT

When viewed from the facilitator paradigm the role of the Holy Spirit in understanding Scripture would not be as direct and mechanical as indicated by the authoritarian paradigm. Yet he would be more proactive than when viewed from the laissez-faire paradigm. The Spirit's participation would not overly dominate that of the reader, yet it would be significant.

In a facilitator paradigm, the Holy Spirit's involvement in illumination would be like that of a teacher who interacts with the student as they together consider challenging material in a textbook. One could imagine the Holy Spirit posing, to the Scripture reader, probing questions regarding the significance of the text's meaning. This would be like the teacher who asks the student questions designed to carry his or her learning experience beyond initial understanding to the point of realizing the implications of what the author is saying in the textbook. In this paradigm the Holy Spirit might go even further by specifically bringing to the reader's awareness the contemporary significance of text; i.e., the theologically consequential message God intends for the reader to understand. This would be like the teacher who not only asks probing questions but also clearly points out to the student the importance and relevance of the author's statements.

---

28. Miller and Seller, *Curriculum*, 111.

29. Moore, *Educational Theory: An Introduction*, 21.

30. Bigge, *Learning Theories for Teachers*, 325.

31. Peterson, "The Christian Teacher," 87.

Summary

Observations concerning the possible role of the Holy Spirit are briefly summarized as follows. In an authoritarian paradigm the Holy Spirit's initiative and proactive stance would make him the dominant participant in hermeneutics. In a laissez-faire paradigm the Holy Spirit would exercise no special initiative. His nonactive stance, that is, his lack of particular and distinctive involvement, would render him practically a nonparticipant in interpretation and exposition. In a facilitator paradigm the Holy Spirit would share a proactive role with the reader in the process of understanding Scripture.

ROLE OF THE RECEIVING AGENTS

Having considered the role of the leading agent (teacher/Holy Spirit), the second step in the proposed analysis and synthesis is to look at the role of the receiving agent (student/reader). The roles of the two agents, though different, are directly related. Thus, in the teacher model, the nature of the student's involvement is seen in relationship to the role the teacher assumes. That is, the nature of the student's role varies depending on whether the teacher's approach is that of the authoritarian, laissez-faire, or facilitator teacher. Correspondingly, when developing a model for illumination from the teacher model, the Scripture reader's role is envisioned distinctively in each of the three basic paradigms.[32]

Authoritarian Paradigm

ROLE OF THE STUDENT

In the authoritarian teacher paradigm the role of the student is usually simply stated. He or she is to be a passive receiver of instructions and information.[33] If the teacher is the repository of knowledge and wisdom, the student is the empty vessel that passively waits to be filled.[34] Thomas J. Sergiovanni and Robert J. Starratt note that in this approach "students

---

32. Again, the reader should note that the titles used to designate the three basic teaching/learning paradigms reflect the teacher's role in the process, rather than that of the student. For consistency and ease of identification, these titles are not changed in the following sections even though the focus of discussion shifts from the role of the leading agent (teacher/Holy Spirit) to that of the receiving agent (student/reader).

33. Bigge, *Learning Theories for Teachers*, 324.

34. Moore, *Educational Theory*, 20.

are subordinate in the sense that they are not partners in the teaching but objects of the teaching."[35] The student is a passive agent and the teacher is an active agent. "The teacher tells and the student listens or the teacher stimulates and the student responds. Thus, this level of teaching is basically uncritical and authoritarian."[36] The teacher plays the strong directive part, and the student's role is merely to respond to the teacher's initiatives. The most important thing that the student can do is focus attention on the teacher and the task of receiving the instructions and information being provided.[37]

ROLE OF THE SCRIPTURE READER

In an authoritarian paradigm, the role of the Scripture reader would be passively to receive understanding from the Holy Spirit. As he or she approached the Scripture, the reader would prayerfully focus his or her attention upon the Holy Spirit and the text. The approach would be like the student who "merely responds to a structured learning situation" and does not exercise much, if any, initiative to consider material other than that provided by the teacher.[38] The reader would carefully consider and meditate upon the text, waiting for the Holy Spirit to enlighten his or her understanding of the material. In the extreme view from this paradigm, the reader's role would be like that in the Ghost-in-a-Machine model discussed above. The Holy Spirit would mysteriously give the interpretation and exposition with little or no effort on the part of the reader.

Laissez-faire Paradigm

ROLE OF STUDENT

The fundamental nature of the student's role in the laissez-faire teacher paradigm is the opposite of that in the authoritarian teacher paradigm. Whereas in the authoritarian paradigm the student is relatively inactive, in the laissez-faire paradigm he or she is expected to be extremely proactive. This corresponds to the laissez-faire teacher's rather indirect, passive-guidance stance. The student follows his or her own initiative.[39]

35. Sergiovanni and Starratt, *Supervision*, 339.

36. Bigge, *Learning Theories for Teachers*, 336.

37. Knight, *Philosophy and Education*, 110.

38. Miller and Seller, *Curriculum*, 56.

39. Bigge, *Learning Theories for Teachers*, 324.

Knight explains that in this approach, the student is not considered to be a passive being who is just waiting for the teacher to pass along information. Rather, the student is a dynamic being who naturally wants to learn and, given the opportunity, is capable of learning on his or her own.[40] Central to the student's role in this paradigm, then, is this conviction that students are "able to carry out their own learning." In keeping with this conviction, Miller and Seller note that those who hold this position assert: "Students should have as much control as possible over their own learning."[41]

Fenstermacher and Soltis emphasize another important feature of the student's role in the laissez-faire paradigm. It is learning by personal experience. They note that learning for the student in this approach is "filled with personal involvement; the whole person is *in* the learning event." Personal involvement "influences every aspect of the learner's being."[42] Carl Rogers, a strong advocate of this approach, uses the term "experiential learning" to capture the essence of the student's role in this paradigm.[43]

ROLE OF THE SCRIPTURE READER

If derived from the laissez-faire paradigm, the reader's role in understanding Scripture would be to put himself or herself actively into the endeavor, not expecting any particular special assistance from the Holy Spirit. Following his or her own initiatives, the reader would delve deeply into the text. He or she would also diligently consider other related material and use any other disciplines that might assist one in understanding the text. The reader would approach the task with the conviction that an understanding of the text could be gained with his or her own abilities and the available tools. Like the student in the laissez-faire teacher paradigm, the reader would expect to learn and gain understanding primarily by his or her own efforts. The reader would expect the Holy Spirit to give little or no direct or special assistance in the endeavor. The emphasis would be upon the reader's own accomplishments in the task.[44]

---

40. Knight, *Philosophy and Education*, 94.

41. Miller and Seller, *Curriculum*, 148, 168.

42. Fenstermacher and Soltis, *Approaches to Teaching*, 30.

43. Rogers, *Freedom to Learn*, 9, 105.

44. As seen above, in the laissez-faire paradigm the assistance that the Holy Spirit would give in understanding Scripture would be only the same general ability that he gives humanity for any other task.

Facilitator Paradigm

ROLE OF THE STUDENT

Upon initial observation, one notes that the role of the student in the facilitator teacher paradigm is quite similar to that in the laissez-faire teacher paradigm.[45] In both of these the student is proactive in comparison to the relatively passive student stance in the authoritarian paradigm. That is, as in the laissez-faire approach, the student in the facilitator approach is not considered to be a passive being who just waits for the teacher to pass along information. Rather, the student actively takes the initiative in the learning endeavor.

For the proactive student, involvement in the learning endeavor is varied. Anita E. Woolfolk, for example, identifies and discusses six specific activities students commonly apply when studying text material: "preview," "question," "read," "reflect," "recite," and "review."[46] Other activities include dialogue with the teacher and responses to the teacher's questions.[47] In dealing with specific problems and questions, the student formulates hypotheses or tentative answers, gathers and evaluates relevant data, and comes to a conclusion.[48] Also, as in the laissez-faire paradigm, learning by personal experience is an essential part of the student's involvement in the facilitator paradigm.[49] The student's participation thus includes a variety of activities that facilitate learning.

Although the student's role in the facilitator paradigm is similar to that in the laissez-faire paradigm, upon closer observation a difference between the two is noted. That difference is at the point of the student's activity in relationship to the activity of the teacher. As seen above, the teacher in the facilitator approach is more proactive than the teacher in the laissez-faire approach. Thus, in the facilitator paradigm, the active participation of both the teacher and the student is a key feature. The emphasis, then, is upon cooperation between the teacher and the student. They mutually share the activities of the teaching/learning task.

45. Moore, *Educational Theory*, 20–21, categorizes models of education into only two prototypes—one in which the student is characterized by "passive reception and imitation," and one in which "the pupil is encouraged to take the initiative."

46. Woolfolk, *Educational Psychology*, 292–93.

47. Eggen et al, *Strategies for Teachers*, 269.

48. Jacobsen et al, *Methods for Teaching*, 162.

49. See Fenstermacher and Soltis, *Approaches to Teaching*, 30, 40–41, 44–45.

The student's role is properly understood only when it is seen in relationship to that of the teacher's and when the participation of both is seen to be essential to the learning process.[50]

ROLE OF THE SCRIPTURE READER

If derived from the facilitator paradigm, the reader's role in understanding Scripture would be characterized by active involvement in cooperation with the Holy Spirit's assistance. The reader would take the initiative to gain understanding about and of the text with whatever available tools and methods. He or she would be like the student who studies text material by surveying, reading, questioning, reflecting, restating, and reviewing. Also, as in a laissez-faire paradigm, the reader would not only delve deeply into the text itself, but would also diligently consider other related material and use other disciplines.

When viewed from the facilitator paradigm, one should especially note that the Scripture reader's role would be understood in relationship to that of the Holy Spirit's. That is, the endeavor of understanding Scripture would be seen as a cooperative task in which the Holy Spirit's participation is essential. The reader would be like the student who relies upon the teacher for insights because "the teacher possesses greater knowledge and has had more experience." The reader would look to the Holy Spirit because, like the teacher, the Holy Spirit is "in a position of being a guide in territory through which he has already passed."[51]

Summary

Concerning the possible roles of the Scripture reader, these points are noted. In an authoritarian paradigm the reader's activity would be minimal since the Holy Spirit would simply "give" understanding of the Scripture. In a laissez-faire paradigm, since the Holy Spirit would not be giving assistance beyond the ordinary, the entire enterprise of hermeneutics would be an ordinary human endeavor. In a facilitator paradigm the reader would share a proactive role in cooperative participation with the Holy Spirit.

---

50. See Miller and Seller, *Curriculum*, 111.

51. Knight, *Philosophy and Education*, 95.

OUTCOMES OR RESULTS OF THE PROCESSES

Having considered both the role of the leading agent (teacher/Holy Spirit) and the role of the receiving agent (student/reader), the third step in this analysis and synthesis is to look at the *outcomes* or *results*. What are the contents and nature of the teaching/learning experience in each of the three teaching paradigms? What do the outcomes of the teaching/learning experience in these paradigms suggest concerning the results of illumination/exposition of Scripture? That is, in what ways do the outcomes observed in teacher/student dynamic indicate the results when the Holy Spirit and the reader interact in the hermeneutical process?

Authoritarian Paradigm

OUTCOMES OF TEACHING/LEARNING

Primarily, the results expected in the authoritarian paradigm are cognitive transference and retention. Moore suggests: "Those who favor this model usually emphasize *what* is to be learned, holding that education involves the pupil in acquiring important knowledge and skills."[52] The goal in this approach is for "specific facts, ideas, topics, or perspectives to be gotten into the heads of the learners."[53] Miller and Seller note that in this paradigm "knowledge is viewed as content." They add: "Knowledge is also seen as something that is relatively 'fixed' and thus can easily be organized into subjects and textbooks."[54] This approach is "most suitable for teaching straightforward subject-matter content," as Sergiovanni and Starratt point out.[55]

Two levels of learning are commonly associated with the authoritarian paradigm: the rote memorization level and the explanatory understanding level. "Memory-level learning is that kind of learning that embraces committing factual materials to memory and nothing else," Bigge writes. Memorized facts contribute indirectly to intelligent behavior only when such facts on occasion become pertinent as usable background in problem solving. Both the memory level and the explanatory level are "basically uncritical and authoritarian." At the explanatory level

---

52. Moore, *Educational Theory*, 20.

53. Fenstermacher and Soltis, *Approaches to Teaching*, 15.

54. Miller and Seller, *Curriculum*, 57.

55. Sergiovanni and Starratt, *Supervision*, 339.

the teacher explains the relationships between generalizations and particulars. Rules and principles are noted; and facts are related to those rules and principles.[56]

RESULTS OF ILLUMINATION/EXPOSITION

The anticipated results of illumination/exposition would be quite easily stated if the authoritarian paradigm were taken as the model. The Holy Spirit would cause the reader to become cognizant of certain facts, ideas, topics, perspectives, rules and principles. He would also help the reader gain some level of understanding the interrelationship of these. Beyond this, the Holy Spirit would also assist the reader to move in understanding from generalizations to particulars.

Keeping in mind that in the authoritarian teacher paradigm the student is relatively passive, one should note that the Scripture reader's understandings would be largely the results of the Holy Spirit's work. As the student who simply receives the information from the teacher and tries to retain it, here the reader would simply be open and receptive to what the Holy Spirit is saying. Out of regard for the authority of the Scripture and the "teacher," the reader would possibly try to memorize important portions of the text. He or she would seek to remember the specific meaning and significance that the Holy Spirit had given to the facts, etc. The reader's level of understanding would be generally limited to the rote and recognition levels as discussed by Richards and others. He or she would know and recognize rather narrowly the information, meaning, and significance conveyed directly to him or her by the Holy Spirit.[57]

When strictly adhered to, the authoritarian approach is limited with regard to its results or outcomes. It is traditionally associated with lower levels of learning. The specific knowledge so valued in this approach denies the student range and depth.[58] "Students may passively absorb content as it is presented by an authority," Bigge notes. However, this "does not carry the quality of experience with it that is needed to enhance the development and use of student intelligence to its fullest potential."[59] Educators have long recognized that if they desire "to move

---

56. Bigge, *Learning Theories for Teachers*, 327–31, 335–36.

57. Richards, *Creative Bible Teaching*, 69–71.

58. See Miller and Seller, *Curriculum*, 59; and Fenstermacher and Soltis, *Approaches to Teaching*, 40.

59. Bigge, *Learning Theories for Teachers*, 337.

students away from being absorbers of information to being processors, synthesizers, creators, and users of information," other teaching methods must be employed.[60] This indicates, then, that the teaching/learning results seen in the authoritarian paradigm do not fully portray the results of the Holy Spirit's activity of illumination. Possibly the laissez-faire and the facilitator paradigms will help contribute to the picture.

Laissez-faire Paradigm

OUTCOMES OF TEACHING/LEARNING

The laissez-faire paradigm is student-centered not only with regard to the role of the student, as seen above, but also with regard to the results of the teaching/learning process. That is, attention is on the person rather than knowledge, on personal growth rather than information, and on creativity rather than conformity.[61] While subject matter is important, in this approach, Peterson says: "The communication of content is low on the priority list."[62]

With this focus on the student, the anticipated outcomes are quite different than those in the authoritarian paradigm. In the laissez-faire paradigm the result is not so much the gaining of information as it is what happens to the individual. "Knowledge is viewed more as process than as content." In this paradigm, "knowledge is viewed as being rooted in personal meaning" rather than "something that is 'fixed' or separate from the individual."[63] This is what Melby refers to as "learning as growth in creativity" and "learning as becoming." The goal of learning is to help the individual become all that he or she is capable of becoming.[64] Those who follow this approach say that learning occurs when the student reaches a high level of self-understanding and self-actualization.[65]

The reader may already notice the existential character of the laissez-faire paradigm. Miller and Seller, who call this position the "transformation position," write: "This paradigm is linked with various forms

---

60. Sergiovanni and Starratt, *Supervision*, 339.

61. See Bigge, *Learning Theories for Teachers*, 327; and Melby, *The Teacher and Learning*, 78.

62. Peterson, "The Christian Teacher," 86.

63. Miller and Seller, *Curriculum*, 168.

64. Melby, *The Teacher and Learning*, 21–25.

65. See Fenstermacher and Soltis, *Approaches to Teaching*, 4.

of mysticism, transcendentalism, and some forms of existentialism." They add: "Learning focuses on integration of the physical, cognitive, affective, and spiritual dimensions."[66] Rogers and other writers emphasize that learning involves the whole being of the individual. It occurs when truth is personally appropriated and assimilated in experience.[67]

Results of Illumination/Exposition

If the laissez-faire paradigm were taken as the model indicating the results of illumination/exposition, one would expect those results to be more than the reader simply understanding certain specific facts, ideas, topics, rules and principles. Scripture would not itself be the message; but rather it would be the medium of the message.[68] That is, the message would not be just the information contained in Scripture but rather the message would be an understanding of what God intends for the particular individual to become. The message would be one of immediate, personal significance to the reader. If learning is learning only when "the learning has personal meaning for the learner,"[69] then, understanding of Scripture is understanding only when the understanding has personal significance for the reader. The results of exposition, according to a laissez-faire paradigm, would be for the reader to understand by experiencing creativity and becoming authentic.[70]

Facilitator Paradigm

Outcomes of Teaching/Learning

Moving from the laissez-faire paradigm to the facilitator paradigm, one notes both differences and similarities in the outcomes of the teaching/ learning process. The results in these two paradigms are different in that those of the laissez-faire paradigm are less definitely defined than those of the facilitator paradigm. In the facilitator paradigm more attention is given to objective content.[71] However, both paradigms are associ-

66. Miller and Seller, *Curriculum*, 167.

67. See Fenstermacher and Soltis, *Approaches to Teaching*, 30; and Rogers, *Freedom to Learn*, 153.

68. See Miller and Seller, *Curriculum*, 59–60.

69. Fenstermacher and Soltis, *Approaches to Teaching*, 30.

70. Ibid., 9, 26, 30.

71. See Fenstermacher and Soltis, *Approaches to Teaching*, 36–37 and general dis-

ated with higher levels of learning. Also, the facilitator teacher seeks to move beyond acquiring objective content. He or she intends to add the subjective element of personal "meaning" or "significance" to the learning process. Learning and knowing are expected to include more than the student simply attaining and retaining certain specified knowledge. Knowing is also experiential. "Learning experiences" and "learning encounters" are characteristic features of the facilitator paradigm.[72]

Educators often seek to identify and describe what is included in higher levels of learning. Bigge associates "exploratory understanding" or the "reflective level" learning with the facilitator paradigm (which he calls the "democratic teacher" approach). At this level, "learning consists of one's either gaining new insights or understandings or changing old ones in an exploratory, experimental method." Bigge describes the "understanding" that occur at this level. He says: "A person understands any object, process, idea, or fact if he sees how it can be used to fulfill some purpose or goal." Further he states: "Understanding occurs when we come to see how to use productively, in ways that we care about, a pattern of general ideas and supporting facts."[73] Sergiovanni and Starratt also discuss learning at higher levels associated with a paradigm in which the teacher functions as "mediator" and/or a "leader." At these levels the student is able to understand more complex concepts, gain higher levels of comprehension, and "extend what is learned to new applications and new situations." Sergiovanni and Starratt note that at this level teaching and learning includes "meaning and significance" and not just "training and conditioning."[74]

RESULTS OF ILLUMINATION/EXPOSITION

If the facilitator paradigm were taken as the model of illumination/exposition, one would expect the reader, with the help of the Holy Spirit, to gain a level of understanding beyond mere information. Succinctly stated, the reader of Scripture would be enabled to realize the meaning and significance as well. Like the student who "sees how it [information] can be used to fulfill some purpose or goal," the Spirit-enlightened reader sees how Scripture's truth can be used to fulfill various purposes or goals.

cussion of these paradigms in other works already cited.

72. Sergiovanni and Starratt, *Supervision*, 322, 339.

73. Bigge, *Learning Theories for Teachers*, 325–27, 332–34, 339.

74. Sergiovanni and Starratt, *Supervision*, 322, 339–42.

In the facilitator paradigm, the results of illumination/exposition, would include the reader realizing how to extend his or her understanding of Scripture to new situations with new and productive applications.

Lawrence O. Richards identifies and discusses five levels of learning that he suggests occurs when Christians teach the Bible. Possibly these may yield insights concerning the outcomes of illumination/exposition. In a facilitator type of teaching/learning approach, Richards sees the student moving beyond the "rote" and "recognition" levels to the "restatement," "relation" and "realization" levels. Correspondingly, if the facilitator paradigm were taken as the model for illumination/exposition, the reader would move beyond the lower levels to the higher levels of understanding Scripture. At the "restatement level" the reader would "have the ability to take a Bible truth, relate it to other ideas and values, and express that truth in [his] own words." At the "relation level" the reader would "see meaning in terms of life," and he or she would be able to identify "the appropriate life-response" to God's Word. The final level of understanding is the experiential level. Richards calls this the "realization level." Here the reader would know by experience in following through with the "appropriate life-response."[75] In this paradigm the Scripture reader would move all the way from a beginning cognitive level of objectively understanding information to an affective level of existentially "knowing" the truth of God.

Summary

Finally, the possible *results* of the hermeneutical process are briefly summarized as follows. In an authoritarian paradigm the Scripture reader's level of understanding would be rather narrowly restricted. The reader would become cognizant of certain information such as facts, perspectives, principles, etc.; and he or she would gain some level of understanding the interrelationships of these.

In a laissez-faire paradigm, knowing would move beyond cognition of information. In the process of becoming the authentic person God intends, the reader would come to an existential understanding of divine truth. One should note that this knowing itself could be said to be metaphysical but the process would not be supernatural since the Holy Spirit would not be giving any assistance beyond the ordinary.

75. Richards, *Creative Bible Teaching*, 69–73.

In the facilitator paradigm, again, knowing would move beyond cognition of information to higher levels. The Scripture reader would gain a level of understanding unique to the experience of making the appropriate life-responses to Scripture's truths. This experiential knowing would be the results of the reader's participation in an extraordinary divine-human cooperative endeavor.

CONCLUSION

From the above analysis, three distinctive models emerge—an authoritarian type, a laissez-faire type, and a facilitator type. Theoretically, any one of the three basic paradigms might be adopted as a model for showing the relationship of the Holy Spirit to the hermeneutical process. All three paradigms are commonly considered to be valid teaching/learning paradigms. Therefore, it seems reasonable that using any one of them as a pattern could result in an illumination/exposition model that would exhibit internal coherence, being intelligible and free from internal self-contradictions. Likewise, their plausibility conceivably could be demonstrated, with each of the three models displaying reasonably logical consistency with truth in general.

Although any one of the three paradigms might be theoretical possibilities, both the authoritarian and the laissez-faire paradigms have potential difficulties. The discussion in chapter 3 indicates that, at least in their distinctive forms, both of these paradigms have primary characteristics that, if followed strictly, would make them largely unacceptable to a majority of theologians. As noted above, an authoritarian model derived from the foregoing analysis is much like the "ghost-in-the-machine" model rejected in chapter 3. This model, if it does not eliminate the need for hermeneutics, at least significantly depreciates its legitimacy. The discussion in chapter 3 likewise indicates that a laissez-faire type of model is also rejected by a majority of present-day scholars. In its most distinctive form as described in the above analysis, this type of model allows little, if any, room for a genuinely vital role of the Holy Spirit. The leading agent in the laissez-faire paradigm is essentially inactive. This pictures well the view that the Holy Spirit, if he plays any role at all in biblical hermeneutics, only assist in some ordinary sense as he would in helping a reader to understand Shakespeare for example. A laissez-faire type of model, then, if it does not eliminate the role of the Holy Spirit in hermeneutics, at least limits it to the ordinary.

While neither the authoritarian nor the laissez-faire paradigms are basically acceptable selections, the facilitator paradigm may provide a fitting model. When the latter paradigm is considered in light of the discussion in chapter 3 some interesting comparisons emerge. Its primary characteristics are strikingly similar to significant features contended for by contemporary scholars who posit a role of the Holy Spirit in hermeneutics. Two points especially need to be noted. One, the facilitator paradigm provides the one model that clearly gives both the Holy Spirit and the Scripture reader genuinely vital roles. Two, this paradigm depicts a hermeneutical model that allows for a broad range of results when the reader seeks to understand Scripture.

Now that the three basic paradigms have been delineated and tentatively evaluated, each one can be made clearer by briefly illustrating them with a Scripture passage example. The reader should keep in mind that in the above descriptions and the following illustrations, the paradigms are purposefully differentiated. Distinguishing attributes have been intentionally featured in order to draw distinctive models. Admittedly, there is a sense in which the authoritarian and laissez-faire paradigms are pictured with extreme characteristics so that clearly distinguishable models emerge. The facilitator paradigm "falls between" the other two and combines some of their characteristics. The following illustrations deliberately attempt to picture the distinguishing characteristics of each paradigm:

> In the beginning was the Word, and the Word was with God, and the Word was God. He was in the beginning with God. All things came into being by Him, and apart from Him nothing came into being that has come into being. In Him was life, and the life was the Light of men. And the Light shines in the darkness, and the darkness did not comprehend it. . . . There was the true Light which, coming into the world, enlightens every man. . . He came to His own, and those who were His own did not receive Him. But as many as received Him, to them He gave the right to become children of God, even to those who believe in His name, who were born not of blood, nor of the will of the flesh, nor of the will of man, but of God. (John 1:1–13)

In the authoritarian paradigm, the reader, being relatively passive, simply meditates intently upon the specified material before him or her and looks to the Holy Spirit for assistance. During this meditation the Holy Spirit, being the proactive agent, tells the reader that the "Word" is Jesus and that Jesus is therefore eternal. The Spirit also tells the reader that there is special significance to the statement that darkness did not overpower Jesus when he came to earth as the "Light." It means that there will come a day when the "Light" of the "Word" will completely eliminate all physical and spiritual "darkness." The Holy Spirit tells the reader that the phrase "enlightens every man" therefore means that ultimately all humanity will be reconciled unto God.

In the laissez-faire paradigm the reader is the proactive agent. He or she studies not only the thirteen verses under consideration, but the rest of this Gospel as well. The reader also relies on grammatical, literary, historical and critical studies in an attempt to discover what the author intended to say. In this study the reader discovers numerous things. For example, he or she learns that the Gospel writer uses the Greek term *Logos* when he refers to Christ as the "Word." The reader objectively considers the customary discussion of this term's usage in Greek thought. He or she concludes that the Gospel writer uses *Logos* here to emphasize God's involvement with his creation in and through Jesus Christ. The reader also learns that the Gospel writer's theme of the struggle between "light" and "darkness" is a motif he shares with the writers of the Qumran community. Evidently, the Gospel writer believes that the *Logos* is victorious or ultimately will be victorious in the struggle. The reader concludes that the Gospel writer is saying that any person can receive the "Light" that the "Word" brings.

According to the laissez-faire paradigm the Holy Spirit is a relatively passive agent. He assists the reader in arriving at the above understandings only in the normal sense that he is an enabler in all human activities. The paradigm would allow, however, that the Holy Spirit may confirm the truth of this passage to the reader and convince him or her of its authoritative character.

In the facilitator paradigm the reader and the Holy Spirit are both proactive when the reader approaches and studies the passage. In this paradigm, the reader studies the materials in the same manner as does the reader in the laissez-faire paradigm described above. He or she would likely reach conclusions and come to understandings which are similar to those of the reader in the laissez-faire paradigm. The difference is that in the facilitator paradigm the Holy Spirit is pictured as also being a proactive participant along with the reader. His role includes something more than being just the ordinary enabler in all human activities. The entire effort is considered to be more of a cooperative enterprise in this paradigm. For example, the Holy Spirit would be especially involved in helping the reader to understand the significance of Jesus being the eternal "Word" and the true "Light." The reader is prayerfully open to the Holy Spirit's enlightenment. In a moment of insight—during the study process—the reader is made profoundly aware of who Jesus really is to those who believe and receive him as the "Word" and "Light." When he or she responds in faith by personally accepting this truth into his or her life, the reader then "knows" something beyond the cognitive level of understanding. He or she "knows" not only *of* or *about* the "Word" and the "Light"; but in personal experience, the reader truly "*knows*" God and the eternal life he gives.

In conclusion, the present writer believes that the facilitator type of teacher model has the greatest potential for serving as a pneumatic hermeneutics paradigm. This paradigm is fundamentally faithful to the Christian tradition. It exhibits internal coherence and logical consistency. Finally, its potential for practical fruitfulness is indicated by its congruence with contemporary positions. The paradigm accurately represents the basic views favored by a majority of scholars who speak to the issue of the Holy Spirit's relationship to hermeneutics.

5

Conclusions and Areas for Further Study

INTRODUCTION

THE INTENT OF THIS study has been to address the questions related to the possible relationship of the Holy Spirit to biblical hermeneutics. The first chapter presented the basic issues and questions. The second chapter surveyed the historical precedents for a role of the Holy Spirit in understanding Scripture. The third chapter described the current views, thereby establishing present positions as a foundation for contemporary understanding of the topic. The fourth chapter suggested a model for extending theological discussion of the Holy Spirit's relationship to the hermeneutical process. With this background, foundation, and model, the study is now ready to offer some conclusions regarding the basic issues and questions raised in the initial chapter.

The focus of this final chapter is twofold. The first section presents the conclusions or results of the study. This is followed by a section that suggests areas for further research.

RESULTS OF THE STUDY

As observed in the introductory chapter, addressing the topic of the Holy Spirit's relationship to hermeneutics is an exercise in philosophical theology. The evidence related to the topic obviously is not easily verifiable, concrete evidence. Therefore, the writer does not claim that the following conclusions can be empirically demonstrated. Given the nature of the topic, such a claim is neither necessary nor fitting. Rather, as in other endeavors to develop theological statements, the conclusions herein are appropriately derived from views that are logically reasonable in the context of related philosophical and theological understandings. Such theological conclusions cannot be proven in a strictly rational sense; but they can be judged to be either plausible or not plausible.

Question of the Spirit's Participation

The initial question encountered in considering the Holy Spirit's relationship to hermeneutics is, of course, the question of whether or not he plays any role in this process. The answer to this question determines the direction of subsequent discussion. That is, if, on the one hand, the answer is, "No," then a certain set of pertaining issues arises. If, on the other hand, the answer is, "Yes," then a different set of issues arises. The findings of this research indicate that the position that says the Holy Spirit does play a role in hermeneutics is the most tenable position. That is, the affirmative, "Yes," answer is the answer that is most logically consistent with other truth.

First, the findings in chapter 2 show the affirmative answer to be in keeping with most of Christian tradition. Testimony of the Early Church Fathers supports this answer. Origen and others of the Alexandrian School, the first major school of biblical interpretation, definitely believed the Holy Spirit had a role, not only in the writing of Scripture, but also in people understanding it. Also, leaders of the Antiochian School, like Chrysostom, and leaders among the Latin Fathers, like Augustine, firmly held that the Holy Spirit was involved in their task of understanding Scripture. In fact, in the church of the Middle Ages, only the scholastics, especially Aquinas, took an approach to biblical understanding that tended to exclude the Holy Spirit.

Likewise, in the Reformation and Post-Reformation era there is overwhelming testimony favoring the affirmative answer. Both Luther and Calvin emphasized the role of the Holy Spirit in understanding Scripture. During this era, Turretin developed Reformed Scholasticism, narrowly confining the work of the Holy Spirit in relationship to Scripture. Yet, even he admitted that Spirit-illumination was necessary for understanding. Also, the English Reformers strongly affirmed the Holy Spirit's role in hermeneutics. Their position was embodied in the first chapter of the famous Westminster Confession. Later confessionalists followed the lead of the Westminster Divines. Owen produced one of the most extensive statements regarding the illumination role of the Holy Spirit ever developed.

During the Enlightenment biblical scholarship moved in significantly different directions. Some of these directions were contrary to traditional views of the Spirit's relationship to the Bible; but in the Post-Enlightenment era there was renewed emphasis on a role of the Holy Spirit in hermeneutics. On the contrary side, Schleiermacher advanced the view that the Bible should be approached hermeneutically just like other ancient writings. Thereafter, Protestant Liberalism (following the leadership of Troeltsch and Bultmann) and Roman Catholic Modernism (following the leadership of Losiy) both made understanding the Bible a purely human enterprise. Likewise, at the opposite end of the theological spectrum, extreme conservative theologians progressively also limited the Holy Spirit's role in hermeneutics. Thus, by the time of Warfield, Fundamentalism's rigorously scholastic approach to Scripture virtually eliminated such a role. Notwithstanding, by the first quarter of the twentieth century, Neo-orthodoxy was once again refocusing attention upon the Holy Spirit's present work in relationship to revelation. Barth, the leading Neo-orthodox theologian, noted the distance between the Bible and human understanding. He strongly reaffirmed the necessity of the Spirit's role in enabling people to understand Scripture.

Therefore, regarding the initial question of this study, the testimony of Christian tradition supports the affirmative answer: "Yes, the Holy Spirit plays a vital role in biblical hermeneutics." True, there have been dissenting voices in all three eras of the church's history defined herein; and the most compelling and sustained objections were raised in the most recent era paralleling the Enlightenment. Nevertheless, overall the majority of church tradition favors the affirmative answer. Also, one of history's clearest and strongest affirmation of the Spirit's role came as a confident, assertive response to the serious objections raised during the Enlightenment.

Second, the position that says the Holy Spirit has a vital role in hermeneutics is also the most tenable one in view of contemporary scholarship. That is, to deny a role of the Holy Spirit in hermeneutics is not only contrary to the majority testimony of church tradition, it is also contrary to present-day witness. As seen in chapter 3, most present-day scholars hold the affirmative position is plausible while to deny the Spirit's role is quite inconsistent with other truth, especially theological tenets.

Christianity stands or falls with its conviction that God is at the same time transcendent and immanent in relationship to his creation.

Transcendence is that whole "other" reality of God beyond creation; immanence is this "other" reality of God constantly being brought into the created order by God himself through revelation. Though God is infinitely above humanity, he is a God of revelation, revealing nothing less than himself to humanity by special revelation in space and time. He is personally active in making himself and his will known to humanity.

To say that God is transcendent and immanent and personally active in making himself know as such, also acknowledges the finitude of humanity and their perennial inability to know God apart from God's constant assistance. This is not to say that humanity has nothing to do with coming to know God and his will. It only means that, although humanity is a participant in the process of revelation, knowing God and his will is never at any time by humanity's initiative or humanity's solitary accomplishment.

The only way that humanity can know God and his will is by God's initiative in revealing himself. The ultimate form of God's special revelation of himself in space and time is the incarnation—the person and work of Jesus Christ. The incarnation is God's immanence personified. In the present discussion one must also note, Christianity holds that the written Word—Scripture—is also special revelation. It reveals God and his plan for humanity's redemption through Jesus Christ.

While Jesus Christ and the written Word are the forms of God's special revelation, God's *activity* of special revelation is called "Spirit." Wolfhart Pannenberg is correct in observing: "Spirit is the name for the actual presence of divine reality in Christian experience." "Thus the idea of spirit allows us to do justice to the transcendence of God and at the same time to explain his immanence in his creation."[1] Thomas F. Torrance expresses the same concept: "Without the Spirit, we have no opening to the transcendent Being, but through the Spirit our concepts are opened in such a way that he is accessible to us." Torrance adds: "He is the creative Agent of God's revelation to us and the creative Agent in our reception and understanding of that revelation."[2]

A word of caution offered by Hans-Georg Gadamer is suggestive of the Spirit's relationship to Scripture. "Interpretation . . . must never forget that scripture is the divine proclamation of salvation. Understanding it, therefore, cannot simply be the scientific or scholarly exploration of

1. Pannenberg, "The Working of the Spirit," 13, 21.

2. Torrance, *God and Rationality*, 168, 188.

its meaning." That is, Scripture, as "a religious proclamation is not there to be understood as a merely historical document, but to be taken in a way in which it exercises it saving effect."[3] Gadamer is surely saying that understanding of Scripture is a salvific activity. Now, if, as Christianity generally agrees, salvific activity is always and at every point a work of the Spirit; then, true understanding of Scripture must be, in some sense, a work of the Spirit.

Holy Spirit illumination of the written Word stands in the larger context of God's entire redemptive activity and the whole process of divine revelation. It is a vital aspect of the Spirit's coming, not to speak of himself, but rather to speak of the Incarnate Word. Without the Holy Spirit, Scripture is a dead letter; but when he uses it to reveal God and his redemption in and through Jesus Christ, it is the living Word of God.

The consensus among a majority of contemporary scholars is that a role of the Holy Spirit in hermeneutics is consistent with the traditional Christian doctrines of God, revelation, and redemption. These scholars shun what Clark Pinnock describes as "the Enlightenment mentality that places most of the emphasis upon academic understanding and minimizes the role of the Spirit in recognizing and interpreting God's Word."[4] Chapter 3 shows that the position of present-day scholars tends to be more like that of the early Reformers and the Westminster Divines. To use the words of Pinnock again, contemporary scholars "rule out a pseudoscientific approach to the text, whether liberal or conservative." Rather, they conclude: "There is a place for Spirit-led interpretation that makes use of the inexhaustible possibilities of the text."[5]

Nature of the Holy Spirit's Role

Answering the initial question in the affirmative—"Yes, the Spirit plays a role in biblical hermeneutics"—immediately raises some subsequent, pertaining issues. One of these is the question: What is the nature of the Holy Spirit's role in the hermeneutical process? That is, if he is a participant, the next question is: *How* does the Holy Spirit enlighten Scripture to the reader's understanding?

---

3. Gadamer, *Truth and Method*, 275, 295.

4. Pinnock, *Scripture Principle*, 155.

5. Ibid., 195

Immediately, the present writer identifies with the difficulty that contemporary scholars have in dealing with these kinds of questions. Pannenberg notes: "It is rather hard to find out what kind of reality one is talking about in referring to the Holy Spirit."[6] Other scholars such as Henry, Torrance, and Ramm agree that illumination, like the other works of the Holy Spirit, is a "mystery." "We know nothing concretely or empirically about such an act," Ramm says.[7] One must admit that since illumination is a divine mystery, the exact *how* of this activity is ultimately beyond finite humanity's ability to describe. If the theologian could describe exactly *how* enlightenment occurs, logically, either he would himself be God or the given activity would be shown not to be a divine "mystery" after all. Humanity's inability at this point is nothing more than the general inadequacy of theology to determine the ultimate mysteries of God.

If Holy Spirit illumination of Scripture is in the final analysis a "mystery," can any thing at all be said concerning *how* he does this work? Chapter 3 shows that while scholars concede: "We know nothing concretely or empirically" about the process; nevertheless, there is a sense in which illumination can be conceptualized and articulated. They claim that, in a way and to an extent, *how* the Holy Spirit enlightens Scripture to the reader's understanding can be described and discussed.

Such a claim is nothing new for theological enterprise. Before he or she even begins, the theologian admits that the endeavors to describe and discuss divine mysteries will lead "far beyond the imaginable." The very nature of the theological task—dealing in knowledge of the invisible, transcendent God—is to imagine and speak about concepts, realities, relationships, and activities which lie above and beyond the imaginable.[8] Janet Martin Soskice is correct in her observation that the Christian theologian always works under the "paradoxical conviction that, despite his utter inability to comprehend God, he is justified in speaking of God."[9]

The *how* of illumination is described and discussed in the same way that theologians generally seek to be articulate about the divine, transcendent order. They rely upon metaphorical language. Following

6. Pannenberg, "The Working of the Spirit," 13.

7. See Ramm, *Witness of the Spirit*, 73.

8. Torrance, *God and Rationality*, 23.

9. Soskice, *Metaphor and Religious Language*, x.

her statement quoted immediately above, Soskice observes that "metaphor is the principle means" by which the theologian imagines and speaks of God and his mysteries. She further explains the relationship between metaphors and models. A "metaphor calls to mind, directly or indirectly, a model or models." For example, "When one says 'the wind howled about the eaves' there is a suggestion that the wind, like a dog or a madman, howls." Since discourse based on models is invariably metaphorical, model and metaphor are closely linked.[10]

As one would expect, the metaphors used to discuss the *how* of illumination follow patterns typical of metaphorical language in general. The Holy Spirit is said to "shine" a light, dispelling the darkness, so that the "eyes" of the reader's mind and heart may be able to "see" the truth. The Spirit serves as a knowledgeable and experienced "guide" to lead in the way of all truth. He is also said to "remove the veil" from people's hearts in order that they may be able to see and understand the truth of Scripture. These metaphors are simply stated without elaboration. Characteristically, brevity is their virtue. Soskice notes: "It is an indication of a good metaphor if it is unnecessary to spell out its implications."[11]

While good metaphors do not need to be elaborated upon, they usually do spontaneously call to mind models that in turn have potential for extending discourse. This is true in the present case especially for the idea of the Holy Spirit "teaching" believers the truths of Scripture. As seen in chapters two and three, "teaching" terminology is the most common metaphorical language used to describe *how* the Holy Spirit illuminates Scripture. Obviously, this metaphor calls to mind a model which pictures the Holy Spirit functioning as a "teacher" in the hermeneutical process.

The present writer believes the "teacher" model provides the best vehicle of discourse on *how* the Holy Spirit illuminates Scripture. A particular method of teaching in biblical times fits well into the facilitator paradigm. That method is the "disciple" method. As a model it also provides some insight into *how* the Holy Spirit—the "Teacher"—helps the reader/student understand the truths of Scripture. J. D. Douglas notes that this kind of "teacher-pupil relationship was a common feature of the ancient world, where Greek philosophers and Jewish Rabbis gathered

10. Ibid., x, 55, 73.

11. Soskice, *Metaphor and Religious Language*, 22–23.

around them groups of apprentices or learners."[12] Jesus, of course, used this method with his followers. "He was the teacher or master; they were his disciples (*mathetai*), a term involving too much personal attachment and commitment to be rendered adequately by 'pupil.'"[13]

In the disciple method, teacher-pupil relationship is an important aspect of the instructional dynamic. The significance of this dynamic as it relates the Holy Spirit's role of teacher of Scripture is seen in Torrance's observation. "We do not know God in the abstract as he is in himself, but only in the reciprocal relation which he has established." Through the Bible or otherwise, the only God people know is the God revealed in the experience of "God-man or man-God relationship."[14] In his discussion of the Holy Spirit's role in hermeneutics, Klooster notes: "God's gracious purpose with this book is to bring about the living 'encounter' with him in an I-thou relationship."[15] *How* the Teacher reveals God and his Truth is by a discipleship type of relationship with the reader.

Like other theological models, the "teacher" model can help one, only up to a point, to envision *how* the Spirit gives understanding of Scripture. Avery Dulles notes: "No theological model can lead to comprehensive knowledge of its subject matter."[16] One must admit that the "teacher" model seeks to provide perception of a reality ultimately too complex and exalted for human comprehension. It is nevertheless beneficial. The extent to which this model is helpful is discussed in chapter 4.

Issue of the Reader's Role

Answering the initial question in the affirmative raises yet another issue. It is the question: How does the Holy Spirit's involvement in the hermeneutical process impact the reader's participation? Another germane way to ask the question is: If the Holy Spirit illuminates Scripture, to what extent, if any, is the studied efforts of the reader essential?

Chapter 3 shows that an overwhelming majority of contemporary scholars contend that the studied efforts of the reader are also essential even though the Holy Spirit illuminates. They deny that the Holy Spirit's

---

12. Douglas, "Disciple," 312.

13. Rayburn, "Names of Christians," 216.

14. Torrance, *God and Rationality*, 31.

15. Klooster, "The Role of the Holy Spirit," 454.

16. Dulles, *Models of Revelation*, 32.

involvement renders the reader's endeavors unnecessary. Rather, they insist on the opposite view. The assistance of the Holy Spirit does not come to a passive mind, but is a supernatural enlightenment to an active one.

The view that pneumatic hermeneutics includes the vital participation of the reader is pictured by the facilitator-type teacher/student model advocated in chapter 4. Taking this model seriously means that for an adequate understanding of Scripture the reader's natural abilities are used to their fullest extent. His native intelligence and talents are greatly enhanced and enriched but in no way obliterated or passed over.[17] Howard M. Ervin is correct in asserting: "Linguistic, literary and historical analysis are indispensable as a first step to an understanding of the Scriptures."[18] The reader's diligent, studied efforts in no way preclude or hinder the Holy Spirit's work of illumination. Such efforts simply mean the reader takes seriously both his role and that of the Holy Spirit.

The view that the human understanding of Scripture is a cooperative endeavor involving the vital participation of both the Holy Spirit and the reader is a plausible position. The two possible alternative views are untenable in light of other commonly held contemporary theological positions. Those two alternative views are: one, deny a role of the Holy Spirit and make hermeneutics a strictly human endeavor; two, make understanding of Scripture an exclusive work of the Holy Spirit and deny any essential human role in interpretation.

To take the first alternative view would make modern critics the ultimate authority on the meaning and significance of the prophetic/apostolic message for today. Carl Henry warns against this. In a discussion specifically on "The Spirit as Divine Illuminator," Henry notes: "It is conceded almost everywhere that recovery of the vitalities of the Spirit is a major Christian imperative."[19] The church is finally recognizing the difficulties associated with its historic problem of an underdeveloped pneumatology. It can now ill afford to accept a pneumatology that excludes the Holy Spirit from the hermeneutical process—a function that is vital to the church's very existence and its mission.

17. The reader should see Abraham, *The Divine Inspiration of Holy Scripture*, 63–64, where Abraham, using a teacher model for inspiration, reaches the same conclusions about the writer's role in the production of Scripture.

18. Ervin, "Hermeneutics," 18.

19. Henry, *God Who Speaks and Shows*, 274, 284.

To take the second alternative view; i.e., to say the Holy Spirit has a role and then deny the essentiality of the reader's role, creates another unacceptable, extreme position. Such a view marks a sharp distinction between the God who addresses us and the Holy Spirit who enables his address to be understood. In the words of John Macquarrie, this view would make the Holy Spirit assume the function of "a mysterious *tertium quid.*"[20]

As the church expands its previously underdeveloped pneumatology, it must avoid both extremes. On the one hand, it must avoid overlooking a role of the Holy Spirit in hermeneutics. On the other hand, it also must avoid making the Holy Spirit some type of enigmatic ghost in the hermeneutical machine. Any view that disavows the essentiality of human scholarly efforts is unacceptable in contemporary biblical studies.

The view of pneumatic hermeneutics that is logically consistent with contemporary theology, then, is the one that not only allows a role of the Holy Spirit but also recognizes the proper role of the reader. As the reader studies, the Holy Spirit illuminates the text. Pinnock states it this way:

> Valid interpretation in the Christian sense must come as a result of fidelity to the text and openness to the Spirit. . . . Not the text by itself, as in Fundamentalism, or the Spirit alone, as in charismatic excesses, but in the fruitful combination of the two.[21]

Anthony C. Thiselton's conclusion is well stated: "The Holy Spirit may be said to work *through* human understanding, and not usually, if ever, through processes which bypass the considerations discussed under the heading of hermeneutics."[22]

Before leaving this topic, two other important aspects of the reader's role need to be summarized. One, when the reader takes the factor of divine involvement seriously, in all of his diligent studied efforts, he is, from beginning to ending, also diligent in prayer and full of faith. He is always prayerfully open to transcendent reality, expecting the Spirit's illumination to make apprehension of that reality possible.

Two, another essential aspect of the reader's role is his response to enlightened understanding. Henry notes: "Those who truly search the

---

20. Macquarrie, *The Scope of Demythologizing*, 50.

21. Pinnock, *The Scripture Principle*, 199.

22. Thiselton, *The Two Horizons*, 92.

Scriptures soon find themselves in the presence of the Great Searcher of souls whom the apostle declares to be also the heavenly explorer of 'the deep things of God' (1 Cor. 2:10, KJV)."[23] Such an encounter, by its very nature, requires a response if the purpose for which it occurs is to be fulfilled. Further, in this encounter—when the reader understands divine truth—his attitude of prayer and faith anticipates not just any response but rather the appropriate one; that is, a positive response.

Therefore, all of the reader's diligent studied efforts, while necessary, by themselves will not gain for him the ultimate understanding of Scripture intended by God. This conclusion is not only in agreement with contemporary views; it is also indicated by the facilitator type of teacher/student model of pneumatic hermeneutics discussed in chapter 4. In that model, hermeneutics is seen to be a cooperative effort between the Holy Spirit and the reader. This means the full fruition of Spirit-illumination is contingent upon the reader's positive response.

The Scripture reader moves beyond an objective level to a subjective level of comprehension precisely in his responses to enlightened understanding of divine truth. This is true because of the very nature and purpose of Scripture as commonly perceived by Christians. Christians commonly hold that Scripture is a special revelation of divine truth given by God especially to accomplish his redemptive purposes in humanity. Those who make a positive response to this revelation experience God's redemption; but those who do not make a positive response do not experience that redemption. Further, to experience God's redemption is to experience God himself in a special sense and on the ultimate level. Thus, in the positive response, one knows and understands divine truth in a special sense and on the ultimate level.[24] But again note that only the reader who positively responds thus knows and understands. Now, if this knowing and understanding occurs during the hermeneutical endeavor, and if the Holy Spirit is an active agent of illumination in the process; then, illumination and positive reader response are inseparably linked.

The reader's response, as can now be seen, is also directly related to the product or results of the Holy Spirit's illumination of Scripture. The reader's response makes a genuine difference in what he understands.

23. Henry, *God Who Speaks and Shows*, 283.

24. Klooster is correct when he states: "Regeneration is the most radical form of illumination one experiences." Klooster, "The Role of the Holy Spirit," 457.

What difference the work of the Holy Spirit makes is the topic of discussion in the next section.

Effects of Illumination on Interpretation/Exposition

What difference does the Holy Spirit's role make? This question is the central and most significant question of this study. The initial question is: Does the Holy Spirit play a role in the hermeneutical process? But what one is really asking is: Does a work of the Holy Spirit make a difference in the outcome when people endeavor to understand Scripture? To answer, "Yes," is to contend that since the Spirit has a vital role, the results will be different than if he did not play such a role. This being the case, then, in what ways or areas is interpretation/exposition affected by illumination of the Holy Spirit?

To contend that a role of the Holy Spirit makes a difference in biblical hermeneutics is to say that there are two aspects of knowing related to understanding Scripture. One aspect is the area of normal intellectual understanding of words, thoughts, facts, and events. This aspect of knowing is achieved by applying objective scientific methods of study. To gain an intellectual knowledge of the biblical material is to understand the ordinary, natural realm of reality as it relates to God, his created order, and his divine plan for humanity. But there is another aspect of knowing related to Scripture. As Alan Richardson says, Scripture also communicates "a knowledge of our 'existence' that is not reached by the processes and methods of objective-scientific thinking."[25] Since this other aspect is of the Spirit and is gained only in cooperation with the Spirit, it is properly called "spiritual" understanding.[26] Fred H. Klooster terms it "heart knowledge" in contrast to head knowledge.[27]

The question is, which of these two aspects of knowing does the illuminating work of the Holy Spirit affect? When contemporary scholars say the Holy Spirit assists the reader in understanding Scripture they appear usually to be speaking of the "spiritual" understanding rather than

---

25. Richardson, *The Bible in the Age of Science*, 104.

26. The reader should note that here the term "spiritual" refers only to things of the Holy Spirit of God. While the sense of the meaning intended includes "divine mysteries" and the "supernatural," it does not include the connotations of "mystical," "magical," or "ghostly."

27. Klooster, "The Role of the Holy Spirit," 455, 457, 462, 463, 466, 468, 471.

the normal intellectual understanding. This position is reasonably based upon the observable phenomena.

Remember, an illuminating work of the Holy Spirit occurring in any aspect of understanding Scripture cannot be empirically demonstrated or rationally proven. "Only the fruits of the Spirit's works are observable," Klooster says.[28] Conclusions regarding illumination, as for other theological positions, are only held to be plausible on the basis of observable phenomena.

Certain observable phenomena can be noted. In the area of normal intellectual understanding, any person with normal intelligence and abilities who applies himself can understand the cognitive content of the Bible in the same way he would understand any other ancient writings. Also note, in effective cooperative endeavors, each participating party has a certain function to perform according to his capabilities. He is not expected to function at a level or in an area beyond his abilities. In genuine cooperative endeavors, however, each participating party is expected to fulfill his vital role with maximum efficiency without expecting the other party to make up for his lack of performance.

One could theorize that God helps readers understand the ordinary cognitive content of the Bible. This would be pictured by the authoritarian type of model discussed in chapter 4. God would certainly be capable of doing this, and in his sovereignty he could certainly choose to do so. However, if pneumatic hermeneutics is a genuinely cooperative endeavor, as advocated above in the facilitator type of model, then it seems reasonable to conclude that ordinary cognitive understanding is the reader's responsibility. One would not usually expect the Holy Spirit to perform this duty for the reader.

Understanding the "spiritual" message of the biblical material is another matter. Christians consider the writings in the Bible to be special divine revelation, "Scripture." To understand its ultimate message is to understand things beyond the normal or natural realm. This aspect of knowing is of the "other" order. Whereas intellectual knowledge is of the ordinary, natural realm, spiritual knowledge is of the transcendent realm. Also, gaining an understanding of the "spiritual" message of Scripture is the product of Holy Spirit enlightenment, herein called "illumination."

---

28. Ibid., 471.

Contemporary scholars use various terms and phrases to identify and delineate this "spiritual" aspect of understanding. Ervin refers to it as the "ultimate word," the "word beyond all human words."[29] Donald G. Bloesch calls it the "revelatory meaning."[30] Torrance calls it "Supreme Truth."[31] In chapter 4 this "spiritual" message of Scripture is termed the "significance," defined as the theologically consequential message that God intends to convey to readers.

When the Holy Spirit helps the reader understand that aspect of the meaning here termed the "significance," what does the reader understand? On the basis of the observable phenomena witnessed by Christians, what the enlightened reader understands can be categorized into two primary components. Obviously, the "significance" includes, as a first component, that basic and general message which is an understanding of God—his character and his plan of redemption of humanity through Jesus Christ. Beyond this basic and general message, however, there is a second component that is personal. When the "Teacher" helps the reader understand the "significance" of Scripture, that message is always intensely personal. The affirmation of contemporary Christians agrees with the testimony of Christians of all ages—the Holy Spirit has a way of relating the message of Scripture to the individual's given situation. Logically, then, there is a sense in which the contemporary "significances" may be as varied as there are individuals who are enlightened by the Spirit.

The fact of varied contemporary "significances" does not, however, imply new meanings or new revelations estranged from the author's original "meaning." Chapter 3 discusses the relationship of Scripture's contemporary "significance" to the author's original "meaning" in his historical situation. The present writer believes Hirsch and others have argued successfully for the position which holds that any valid understanding of a text is directly related to the original "meaning" and does not contradict the author's intention.[32] Henry states a balanced view. The Holy Spirit "stretches" the author's meaning to give the text contemporary significances that need not have been consciously intended

29. Ervin, "Hermeneutics," 16.

30. Bloesch, "A Christological Hermeneutic," 100.

31. Torrance, *God and Rationality*, 186.

32. The reader should see, Hirsch, *Validity in Interpretation*; and Hirsch, *The Aims of Interpretation*.

by the author. Yet, Henry concludes that these are "not contrary to the writer's intention."[33] There is a line of continuity between the original "meaning" of Scripture and any contemporary meaning, here termed, the "significance."[34]

How may the "spiritual" message of Scripture be further delineated? The claim has been made above that the "significance" includes that basic and general message which is an understanding of God—his character and his plan of redemption through Jesus Christ. This basic and general component consists of much more than simply knowledge *about* God. When the Holy Spirit illuminates Scripture he reveals none other than the being of God himself. "God communicates not something of himself, nor just something about himself, but himself," Torrance says. Thus, when the reader truly comprehends "Supreme Truth," he not only knows about God—he knows God himself personally. "With the coming of the Spirit to us the being of God Almighty . . . breaks through the distance between the creature and the Creator, . . . disclosing himself to us personally."[35]

This emphasis upon the Holy Spirit revealing the being of God in Scripture does not imply a dichotomy between knowing about God on the one hand and knowing God himself on the other hand. The written revelation of God in Scripture is true information from and about God. Certainly, a reader can learn *about* God from the Bible without knowing God himself. However, when enlightenment occurs, if the reader responds positively, the Holy Spirit simply uses the information about God to reveal the Being of God himself.[36] This is the essence of the Spirit's work of illuminating the written Word—revealing the being of God.

Another important point can now be made. In its final outcome, pneumatic hermeneutics is by its very nature and in its ultimate objective christological. This conclusion follows from the discussion of contemporary positions in chapter 3. Present-day scholars recognize that when the Holy Spirit illuminates Scripture and the reader truly knows

33. Henry, *God Who Speaks and Shows*, 281.

34. Autry notes: "Evangelicals have argued most strenuously for the importance of the correct reading [the author's meaning], without which any creative reading [significance] has dubious value." He says interpreters should not be forced to choose between "correct" and "creative," concluding: "To choose either against the other is to impoverish the Bible's role in the church." See Autry, "The Five Dimensions of Hermeneutics," 2.

35. Torrance, *God and Rationality*, 172–73, 179, 186.

36. See Richards, *Creative Bible Teaching*, 52–53, 56.

the meaning and significance of its message, what he understands is God's disclosure of himself in and through Jesus Christ. Wilhoit states it clearly and concisely: "The Holy Spirit uses Scripture to witness to and glorify Jesus Christ."[37]

The christological nature and purpose of pneumatic hermeneutics is not surprising since, in light of the incarnation event, both hermeneutics and pneumatology must be christological in character and objective. Christians commonly agree that the incarnation means the supreme revelation of God himself *is* Jesus Christ. The person and work of Jesus Christ is the perfect presentation of the loving, redemptive character and activity of God. The New Testament writers express this idea. The writer in Col 1:15 says: "[Jesus Christ] is the image of the invisible God." The writer in Heb 1:3 says: "[Jesus Christ] is the radiance of [God's] glory and the exact representation of [God's] nature." Bloesch, along with others, is correct, then, in calling for a "christological hermeneutic" in which "the innermost intentions of the author are related to the center and culmination of sacred history mirrored in the Bible, namely, the advent of Jesus Christ." God reveals himself fully and definitively in the life history of Jesus Christ. "This revelation was anticipated in the Old Testament and remembered and proclaimed in the New Testament," Bloesch says.[38]

In light of the incarnation, pneumatology is also christological in character and objective. That is, as understood from John 16:13–15, the very purpose for which the Holy Spirit is sent into the world is to speak of Jesus Christ. Ramm notes: "The intense christological character of the pneumatology of the New Testament is stated in John 16:14."[39] In this verse, the Gospel writer refers to Jesus as saying concerning the Holy Spirit: "He shall glorify me; for he shall take of mine, and shall disclose it to you." Ultimately, then the role of the Holy Spirit in biblical hermeneutics is directly related to the primary purpose for which he is sent into the world; i.e., to glorify and disclose Jesus Christ.

AREAS FOR FURTHER STUDY

In view of the above observations and conclusions at least three areas for further study emerge:

37. Wilhoit, *Christian Education and the Search for Meaning*, 49.

38. Bloesch, "A Christological Hermeneutic," 81–82.

39. Ramm, *Witness of the Spirit*, 58.

(1) Chapter 4 suggests that extrapolations can be made from the idea that teaching/learning is a paradigm for illumination/exposition. That is, in the hermeneutical process, the Holy Spirit functions like a teacher in a teaching/learning situation. In the above presentation, some of the observations and conclusions are based on such extrapolations as indicated in the discussion. However, no claim is made that the process is herein exhausted. This strategy needs to be extended by theological scholars with expertise in epistemology and learning theory.

Possibly a thoroughgoing eclectic model would emerge as these paradigms are considered more closely. Although the facilitator type is held to be the one best paradigm, an eclectic model composed of features from all three teacher paradigms might be more fruitful. Writing about these basic paradigms, Fenstermacher and Soltis suggest: "Each of these three approaches contain something of value."[40] Secular and religious educators generally observe that the most effective teachers are those who use a variety of teaching methods. Judging the Holy Spirit to be an effective "teacher," one could easily envision him using methods from all three approaches.

For example, an eclectic model could include the following characteristics. Such a model might emphasize the activity of an omniscient Holy Spirit more than does the facilitator paradigm alone. This is because the authoritarian paradigm features the teacher as the authority who possesses knowledge of value to the student. He or she freely shares this knowledge with the student. An eclectic model might place more emphasis on the motivational role of the Spirit since the laissez-faire teacher is especially known as a motivator. Drawing from the authoritarian paradigm, an eclectic model would feature the reader intently focusing attention upon the Scripture text and prayerfully expecting the Holy Spirit's help. However, in keeping with the laissez-faire paradigm, the reader, while anticipating the Spirit's assistance, would not presume upon his aid. The reader would take the initiative to engage in serious study of the text and related materials almost as though the entire outcome depended upon his or her efforts. These emphases are not necessarily incompatible with the mutual cooperative aspect of the facilitator paradigm. Additional features, drawn from the other two paradigm, could

---

40. Fenstermacher and Soltis, *Approaches to Teaching*, 55.

also be integrated with the characteristics of the facilitator paradigm in order to form an eclectic model.

(2) Early in chapter 3 the question was raised as to why many hermeneuts and hermeneutical systems do not include and discuss a role of the Holy Spirit. This question was briefly considered, but it needs to be explored further. What are the implications of such an omission? Does it mean that a role of the Holy Spirit is incompatible with or contrary to their approach to Scripture? Or, does it means the question of the Holy Spirit's relationship to the given hermeneutical system simply has not been raised and discussed adequately?

Obviously, in some cases the answer is clearly that a role of the Holy Spirit is contrary to the given approach. For example, as observed above, this is the case for both Schleiermacher's and Bultmann's hermeneutics. Schleiermacher's "no separate hermeneutics for the Bible" and Bultmann's "history as a closed continuum," by their design, both leave the Holy Spirit out of the "hermeneutical circle." Also, a rigorously scholastic approach like that of the latter Princeton theologians and recent fundamentalists eliminates a role of the Holy Spirit in hermeneutics.

For other hermeneutical approaches the answer to the question of the Holy Spirit's involvement is not yet clearly answered. It is in these cases that further research is needed. Two hermeneutical methods will serve as examples. "The New Hermeneutic," though developed by followers of Bultmann such as Ernst Fuchs and Gerhard Ebeling, appears to include a role of the Holy Spirit. Thiselton says: "Fuchs and Ebeling are fully aware of the role of the Holy Spirit in communicating the word of God."[41] However, a search of their writings reveals only limited specific references to the Holy Spirit's relationship to their approach. Ebeling warns against "invoking the aid of the Holy Spirit too early in the discussion." He also declares: "The Holy Spirit, which is the Spirit of the Word, . . . is concerned with everything which has to do with the word-event."[42] Such statements appear to suggest a role of the Holy Spirit. However, the lack of further specific discussion leaves the question yet to be definitely answered. Perhaps further study could determine to what extent

41. Thiselton, "The New Hermeneutic," 309.

42. Ebeling, *Theology and Proclamation*, 42, 102.

a teacher-paradigm role of the Holy Spirit could be integrated into the other elements of the New Hermeneutic.

The other example is "Reader-response Criticism." This approach is a 1960s and 1970s development of secular literary studies and is only recently being brought to biblical hermeneutics. The initial advocates of this method obviously had little or no interest in the issue of a role of the Holy Spirit in understanding literary pieces. Those who are seeking to adapt reader-response criticism to biblical studies have yet to consider the relationship of the Holy Spirit to this system. The present writer sees two areas where the idea of the Spirit's role in hermeneutics may have affinity to elements of reader-response criticism. One, both the idea of the Spirit's role and reader-response criticism emphasize the subjective aspect of understanding literature. Two, obviously the reader's response is a key factor according to reader-response criticism. The present study on the Holy Spirit's relationship to biblical hermeneutics suggests that response is also essential to the reader's understanding of Scripture. Further research could determine whether there are other points of commonality.

(3) There is a need for extensive exegetical study to establish a biblical basis for a role of the Spirit in understanding Scripture. At various places throughout this study certain Scripture texts have been cited or referred to in relationship to the discussion. Chapter 4 applies a Scripture passage example to each of the three teacher paradigms to illustrate the Holy Spirit's relationship to the hermeneutical process as pictured in each of these models. Beyond these uses of Scripture, however, extensive exegetical study could be helpful.

There are several references in the Bible to the general idea of God being the one who "teaches" truth to humanity. For example, the author of Ps 94:12 writes: "Blessed is the man whom Thou dost chasten, O Lord, and dost teach out of Thy law." References in both the Old Testament and New Testament associate this teaching activity more specifically with the Holy Spirit. Nehemiah 9:20 says, "Thou didst give them thy good Spirit to instruct them." In Ps 143:10 the Psalmist asks of God: "Teach me to do thy will, . . . let thy good Spirit lead me." The author of John 14:26 writes: "But the helper, the Holy Spirit, whom the Father will send in My name, He will teach you all things, . . ." Exegetical study could help answer the question:

Do these and other passages in the Bible indicate and support the idea of the teacher model being a paradigm for illumination/exposition?

Two other New Testament passages especially need to be more thoroughly considered. A text often discussed in the literature on Holy Spirit illumination is 1 Cor 2:10–15. Verses 11 and 13 indicate that the writer has a teacher model in mind. Another text often cited is 2 Cor 3:5–17, a passage that depicts the results of the Spirit's teaching ministry. To what extent do these passages describe the Holy Spirit's relationship to hermeneutics?

CONCLUSION

The question of the Holy Spirit's relationship to biblical hermeneutics is a crucial question. Christians commonly believe the Bible is special revelation. Further, they believe that correct and complete understanding of it in today's context is important to the individual as well as the Christian community as a whole. Logically, the question of whether or not the Holy Spirit plays a role in gaining that understanding could be quite significant.

On this question, the present writer agrees with the majority of contemporary scholars—to hold that the Holy Spirit plays a vital role in the hermeneutical process is a tenable position. This conclusion is based upon historical, philosophical, and theological arguments and the observable phenomena as presented above. It means the human understanding of Scripture is a cooperative enterprise involving the help of the Holy Spirit and the diligent efforts of the reader. The unique roles of both the Holy Spirit and the reader make a genuine difference in the outcome of the endeavor.

In the present age of the church there is a renewed awareness of the importance of biblical hermeneutics. Also, the church is now accepting the long neglected challenge of developing a mature pneumatology. In this climate, scholars have a unique opportunity to consider the relationship of the Holy Spirit to hermeneutics. A keen awareness of and proper response to the Holy Spirit's role is essential to receiving and appropriating from Scripture God's message for today.

Bibliography

Abraham, William J. *The Divine Inspiration of Holy Scripture.* Oxford: Oxford University Press, 1981.

Alexander, Archibald. "Inaugural Address." In *The Princeton Theology, 1812-1921: Scripture, Science, and Theological Method from Archibald Alexander to Benjamin Warfield,* ed. and comp. Mark A. Noll. Grand Rapids, MI: Baker, 1983.

Allison, Leon McDill. "The Doctrine of Scripture in the Theology of John Calvin and Francis Turretin." Th.M. thesis, Princeton Theological Seminary, 1958.

Aquinas, Thomas. *The Existence of God.* Translated by the Blackfriars. Vol. 1 of *Summa Theologiae,* ed. Thomas Gilby. New York: Image, 1969.

Augustine. *Anti-Pelagian Writings.* Vol. 5 of *A Select Library of the Nicene and Post-Nicene Fathers of the Christian Church,* ed. Philip Schaff. Grand Rapids, MI: Eerdmans, 1956.

———. *City of God* and *On Christian Doctrine.* Translated by J. F. Shaw. Vol. 2 of *A Select Library of the Nicene and Post-Nicene Fathers of the Christian Church,* ed. Philip Schaff. Grand Rapids, MI: Eerdmans, 1956.

———. *The Confessions of Saint Augustin.* Translated by J. G. Pilkington. Vol. 1 of *A Selected Library of the Nicene and Post-Nicene Fathers of the Christian Church,* ed. Philip Schaff. Grand Rapids, MI: Eerdmans, 1956.

———. *Of the Work of Monks.* Translated by H. Browne. Vol. 3 of *A Select Library of the Nicene and Post-Nicene Fathers of the Christian Church,* ed. Philip Schaff. Grand Rapids, MI: Eerdmans, 1956.

Autry, Arden C. "The Five Dimensions of Hermeneutics." Manuscript written at Oral Roberts University, 1985. Copy in Moody Memorial Library, Baylor University, Waco, Texas.

———. "The Spiritual Man and Understanding: I Corinthians 2:14–15." Manuscript presented to alumni of the Theology Department, Oral Roberts University, 1986. Copy in Moody Memorial Library, Baylor University, Waco, Texas.

Barbour, Ian G. *Myths, Models, and Paradigms.* New York: Harper and Row, 1974.

Barclay, William. *The Promise of the Spirit.* Philadelphia: Westminster, 1960.

Barth, Karl. *The Doctrine of the Word of God.* Translated by G. T. Thomson and Harold Knight. Vol. 1.2 of *Church Dogmatics,* eds. G. W. Bromiley and T. F. Torrance. Edinburg: Clark, 1956.

———. *The Epistle to the Romans.* 6th ed. Translated by Edwyn C. Hoskyns. London: Oxford University Press, 1933; reprint, London: Oxford University Press, 1980.

Battles, Ford Lewis. "God Was Accommodating Himself to Human Capacity." *Int* 31 (January 1977) 19–38.

Baur, Chrysostomus. *John Chrysostom and His Times.* Westminster, Maryland: Newman, 1959.

Behm, Johannes. "*Hermeneuo.*" In *TDNT.*

Berkhof, Louis. *Principles of Biblical Interpretation*. Grand Rapids, MI: Baker, 1952.

Berkouwer, G. C. *Holy Scripture*. SDS. Grand Rapids, MI: Eerdmans, 1975.

Bigge, Morris L. *Learning Theories for Teachers*. 3rd ed. New York: Harper and Row, 1976.

Black, Max. *Models and Metaphors: Studies in Language and Philosophy*. Ithaca, New York: Cornell University Press, 1962.

Bleicher, Josef. *Contemporary Hermeneutics: Hermeneutics as Method, Philosophy and Critique*. London: Routhledge and Kegan Paul, 1980.

Bloesch, Donald G. "A Christological Hermeneutic: Crisis and Conflict in Hermeneutics." In *The Use of the Bible in Theology: Evangelical Options*, ed. Robert K. Johnson. Atlanta: John Knox, 1985.

———. *Essentials of Evangelical Theology*. New York: Harper and Row, 1978.

———. "The Sword of the Spirit: The Meaning of Inspiration." *RefR* 33 (Winter 1980) 65–72.

Braaten, Carl E. *History and Hermeneutics*. Vol. 2 of *New Directions in Theology Today*, ed. William Hordern. Philadelphia: Westminster, 1966.

Breck, John. "Exegesis and Interpretation: Orthodox Reflections on the 'Hermeneutical Problem.'" *SVTQ* 27 (1983) 75–92.

Bromiley, Geoffrey W. "The Church Fathers and Holy Scripture." In *Scripture and Truth*, eds. D. A. Carson and John D. Woodbridge. Grand Rapids, MI: Zondervan, 1983.

———. "The Interpretation of the Bible." In vol. 1 of *EBC*.

Brown, Colin. "The Enlightenment." In *EDT*.

Brown, Raymond Edward. *The Sensus Plenior of Sacred Scripture*. Baltimore: St. Mary's University, 1955.

Bruce, F. F. "Interpretation of the Bible." In *EDT*.

Bullock, C. Hassell. "Introduction: Interpreting the Bible." In *The Literature and Meaning of Scripture*, ed. Morris A. Inch and C. Hassell Bullock. Grand Rapids, MI: Baker, 1981.

Calvin, John. *Commentaries on the Catholic Epistles*. Translated by John Owen. Grand Rapids, MI: Eerdmans, 1948.

———. *Commentaries on the Epistles of Paul the Apostle to the Philippians, Colossians, and Thessalonians*. Translated by John Pringle. Grand Rapids, MI: Eerdmans, 1948.

———. *Commentary on the Acts of the Apostles*, vols. 1 and 2. Translated by Christopher Fetherstone. Grand Rapids, MI: Eerdmans, 1949.

———. *Commentary on the Book of Psalms*, vol 5. Translated by James Anderson. Grand Rapids, MI: Eerdmans, 1949.

———. *Commentary on the Epistles of Paul the Apostle to the Corinthians*, vol. 1. Translated by John Pringle. Grand Rapids, MI: Eerdmans, 1948.

———. *Institutes of the Christian Religion*. 2 vols. Translated by John Allen. 7th Am. ed. Revised by Benjamin B. Warfield. Philadelphia: Presbyterian Board of Christian Education, 1936.

Chrysostom, John. *Homilies on the Epistles of Paul to the   Corinthians*. Translated by Talbot W. Chambers. Vol. 12 of *A Selected Library of the Nicene and Post-Nicene Fathers of the Christian Church*, ed. by Philip Schaff. Grand Rapids, MI: Eerdmans, 1956.

———. *Homilies on the Gospel of Saint John*, part I. Translated by members of the English Church. In *A Library of Fathers of the Holy Catholic Church*. London: Rivington, 1848.

———. *Homilies on the Gospel of Saint John and the Epistle to the Hebrews.* The Oxford Translation. Vol. 14 of *A Selected Library of the Nicene and Post-Nicene Fathers of the Christian Church*, ed. Philip Schaff. Grand Rapids, MI: Eerdmans, 1956.

DeVenny, Thomas Alston. "The Holy Spirit as the Interpreter of the Old Testament in the New Testament Community." Ph.D. diss., Southern Baptist Theological Seminary, 1961.

Douglas, J. D. "Disciple." In *NBD*.

Dulles, Avery. *Models of Revelation.* Garden City, New York: Doubleday, 1983.

Dunnett, Walter M. *The Interpretation of Holy Scripture.* New York: Thomas Nelson, 1984.

Ebeling, Gerhard. *Theology and Proclamation: Dialogue with Bultmann.* Translated by John Riches. Philadelphia: Fortress, 1966.

Eggen, Paul D., Donald P. Kauchak and Robert J. Harder. *Strategies for Teachers.* Englewood Cliffs, NJ: Prentice-Hall, 1979.

Elwell, Walter A., ed. *Evangelical Dictionary of Theology.* Grand Rapids, MI: Baker, 1984.

Erickson, Millard J. *Christian Theology.* Grand Rapids, MI: Baker, 1985.

Ervin, Howard M. "Hermeneutics: A Pentecostal Option." *Pneuma* 3 (Fall 1981) 11–25.

Farrar, Frederic W. *History of Interpretation.* E. P. Dutton, 1886; reprint, Grand Rapids, MI: Baker, 1961.

Fee, Gordon D. "The Genre of New Testament Literature and Biblical Hermeneutics." In *Interpreting the Word of God*, eds. Samuel J. Schultz and Morris A. Inch. Chicago: Moody, 1976.

Fee, Gordon D. and Douglas Stuart. *How to Read the Bible for all Its Worth: A Guide to Understanding the Bible.* Grand Rapids, MI: Zondervan, 1982.

Fenstermacher, Gary D. and Jonas F. Soltis. *Approaches to Teaching.* Thinking about Education Series, ed. Jonas F. Soltis. New York: Teachers College, 1986.

Forstman, H. Jackson. *Word and Spirit: Calvin's Doctrine of Biblical Authority.* Stanford, CA: Stanford University Press, 1962.

Fuller, Daniel P. "The Holy Spirit's Role in Biblical Interpretation." In *Scripture, Tradition, and Interpretation*, eds. W. Ward Gasque and William Sanford LaSor. Grand Rapids, MI: Eerdmans, 1978.

Funk, Robert W. *Language, Hermeneutic, and the Word of God.* New York: Harper and Row, 1966.

Gadamer, Hans-Georg. *Reason in the Age of Science.* Translated by Frederick G. Lawrence. Cambridge: Massachusetts Institute of Technology Press, 1981.

———. *Truth and Method.* New York: Seabury, 1975.

German, T. J. "Scholasticism." In *EDT*.

Grant, Robert and David Tracy. *A Short History of the Interpretation of the Bible.* 2nd ed. Philadelphia: Fortress, 1984.

Grech, Prosper. "The 'Testimonia' and Modern Hermeneutics." *NTS* 19 (April 1973) 318–24.

Greidanus, Sidney. *The Modern Preacher and the Ancient Text: Interpreting and Preaching Biblical Literature.* Grand Rapids, MI: Eerdmans, 1988.

Gruenler, R. G. "The New Hermeneutic." In *EDT*.

Harrington, Daniel J. *Interpreting the New Testament: A Practical Guide.* New Testament Message Series, ed. Wilfird Harrington and Donald Senior. Wilmington, DE: Michael Glazier, 1979.

Hasel, Gerhard F. *New Testament Theology: Basic Issues in the Current Debate*. Grand Rapids, MI: Eerdmans, 1978.

———. *Old Testament Theology: Basic Issues in the Current Debate*, 3rd ed. Grand Rapids, MI: Eerdmans, 1972.

Henry, Carl F. H. *God Who Speaks and Shows*. Vol. 4 of *God, Revelation and Authority*. Waco, TX: Word, 1970.

Hirsch, E. D., Jr. *The Aims of Interpretation*. Chicago: University of Chicago Press, 1976.

———. "Current Issues in Theory of Interpretation." *JR* 55 (July 1975) 298–312.

———. *Validity in Interpretation*. New Haven, CT: Yale University Press, 1967.

Hodge, Charles. *Systematic Theology*. 3 Vols. New York: Scribner, Armstrong and Co., 1874; reprint, Grand Rapids, MI: Eerdmans, 1986.

Hoffman, Thomas A. "Inspiration, Normativeness, Canonicity, and the Unique Sacred Character of the Bible." *CBQ* 44 (1982) 447–69.

Hughes, Philip E. *The Second Epistle to the Corinthians*. NICNT. Grand Rapids, MI: Eerdmans, 1982.

Jacobsen, David, et al. *Methods for Teaching: A Skills Approach*. London: Charles E. Merrill, 1981.

Johnson, W. W. "The Ethics of Preaching." *Int* 20 (Oct. 1966) 412–31.

Kaiser, Walter C., Jr. "Legitimate Hermeneutics." In *Inerrancy*, ed. Norman L. Geisler. Grand Rapids, MI: Zondervan, 1977.

Kasper, Walter. "Roman Catholic Theology." In *WDCT*.

Keegan, Terence J. *Interpreting the Bible*. New York: Paulist, 1985.

Klooster, Fred H. "The Role of the Holy Spirit in the Hermeneutic Process: The Relationship of the Spirit's Illumination to Biblical Interpretation." In *Hermeneutics, Inerrancy, and the Bible*, eds. Earl D. Radmacher and Robert D. Preus. Grand Rapids, MI: Zondervan, 1984.

Knight, George R. *Philosophy and Education*. Berrien Springs, MI: Andrews University Press, 1980.

Kraus, Hans-Joachin. "Calvin's Exegetical Principles." *Int* 31 (January 1977) 8–18.

Krentz, Edgar. *The Historical-Critical Method*. GBS. Philadelphia: Fortress, 1975.

LaSor, William Sanford. "Prophecy, Inspiration, and *Sensus Plenior*." *TynBul* 29 (1978) 49–60.

Lee, James Michael. "The Authentic Source of Religious Instruction." In *Religious Education and Theology*, ed. Norma H. Thompson. Birmingham: Religious Education Press, 1982.

Leschert, Dale. "Inspired Hermeneutics? A Study in the Validity of Inspired New Testament Interpretation." Master thesis, Western Conservative Baptist Seminary, 1981.

Lockman Foundation. *New American Standard Bible*. London: Cambridge University Press, 1960.

Loisy, Alfred. *The Gospel and the Church*. Translated by Christopher Home. New York: Scribner, 1912.

———. *The Origins of the New Testament*. Translated by L. P. Jacks. New York: Macmillan, 1950.

Luther, Martin. *Lectures on Genesis Chapters 15–20*. Translated by George V. Schick. Vol. 3 of *Luther's Works*, eds. Jaroslav Pelikan and Daniel E. Poellot. Saint Louis: Concordia, 1961.

———. *Selected Psalms II*. Translated by Martin H. Bertram. Vol. 13 of *Luther's Works*, eds. Jaroslav Pelikan and Daniel E. Poellot. Saint Louis: Concordia, 1956.

———. *Selected Psalms III*. Translated by Jaroslav Pelikan. Vol. 14 of *Luther's Works*, eds. Jaroslav Pelikan and Daniel E. Poellot. Saint Louis: Concordia, 1958.

———. *Sermons on the Gospel of St. John, Chapters 1–4*. Translated by Martin H. Bertram. Vol. 22 of *Luther's Works*, eds. Jaroslav Pelikan and Daniel E. Poellot. Saint Louis: Concordia, 1957.

———. *Sermons on the Gospel of St. John, Chapters 6–8*. Translated by Martin H. Bertram. Vol. 23 of *Luther's Works*, eds. Jaroslav Pelikan and Daniel E. Poellot. Saint Louis: Concordia, 1959.

Macquarrie, John. *The Scope of Demythologizing: Bultmann and His Critics*. The Library of Philosophy and Theology Series. London: SCM Press, 1960.

Marsh, F. E. *The Structural Principles of the Bible or How to Study the Word of God*. Grand Rapids, MI: Kregel, 1969.

McDonald, H. D. *Theories of Revelation: An Historical Study, 1860–1960*. London: George Allen and Unwin, 1963.

McIntire, C. T. "Vatican Council II." In *EDT*.

McKim, Donald K. ed., *A Guide to Contemporary Hermeneutics: Major Trends in Biblical Interpretation*. Grand Rapids, MI: Eerdmans, 1986.

McLean, Mark D. "Toward a Pentecostal Hermeneutic." *Pneuma* 6 (Fall 1984) 35 –56.

Melby, Ernest O. *The Teacher and Learning*. Washington, DC: The Center for Applied Research in Education, 1963.

Mickelsen, A. Berkely. *Interpreting the Bible*. Grand Rapids, MI: Eerdmans, 1985.

Miller, John P. and Wayne Seller. *Curriculum: Perspectives and Practices*. New York: Longman, 1985.

Montague, George. *The Holy Spirit: Growth of a Biblical Tradition*. New York: Paulist, 1976.

Moore, T. W. *Educational Theory: An Introduction*. London: Routledge and Kegan Paul, 1974.

Morgan, Robert. *Introduction to Ernst Troeltsch: Writings on Theology and Religion*, eds. Robert Morgan and Michael Pye. Atlanta: John Knox, 1977.

Mudge, Lewis S. "Hermeneutics." In *WDCT*.

———. "Infallible Scripture and the Role of Hermeneutics." In *Scripture and Truth*, eds. D. A. Carson and John D. Woodbridge. Grand Rapids, MI: Zondervan, 1983.

Mueller, David L. *Karl Barth*. Makers of the Modern Theological Mind Series, ed. Bob E. Patterson. Waco, TX: Word Books, 1972.

Mueller-Vollmer, Kurt. *Preface to The Hermeneutics Reader: Texts of the German Tradition from the Enlightenment to the Present*, ed. Kurt Mueller-Vollmer. New York: Continuum, 1985.

Murray, John. *Calvin as Theologian and Expositor*. London: The Evangelical Library, 1964.

Nash, Ronald. *The Word of God and the Mind of Man*. Grand Rapids, MI: Zondervan, 1982.

Neill, Stephen. *The Interpretation of the New Testament: 1861–1961*. Oxford: Oxford University Press, 1964.

Noll, Mark A. *Introduction to The Princeton Theology, 1812-1921: Scripture, Science, and Theological Method from Archibald Alexander to Benjamin Breckinridge Warfield*, ed. Mark A. Noll. Grand Rapids, MI: Baker, 1983.

Origen. *An Exhortation to Martyrdom, On Prayer, On First Principles: Book IV, The Prologue to the Commentary on The Song of Songs, Homily XXVII on Numbers.* Translated by Rowan A. Greer. CWS. New York: Paulist, 1979.

Origen. "De Principiis." In *Fathers of the Third Century.* Vol. 4 of *The Ante-Nicene Fathers,* eds. Alexander Roberts and James Donaldson. New York: Schribner, 1913.

Owen, John. *Works.* 17 vols. Edited by William H. Goold. London: Johnstone and Hunter, 1852.

Pache, Rene. *The Inspiration and Authority of Scripture.* Translated by Helen I. Needham. Chicago: Moody, 1969.

Packer, James I. "Contemporary Views of Revelation." In *Revelation and the Bible,* ed. Carl F. H. Henry. Grand Rapids, MI: Baker, 1958.

Palma, Anthony D. *The Spirit—God in Action.* Springfield, MO: Gospel Publishing House, 1974.

Palmer, Richard E. *Hermeneutics: Interpretation Theory in Scleiermacher, Dilthey, Heidegger, and Gadamer.* Evanston, IL: Northwestern University, 1969.

Pannenberg, Wolfhart. "The Working of the Spirit in the Creation and in the People of God." In *Spirit, Faith, and Church.* The 1969 Walter and Mary Tuohy Chair Lectures, ed. Edward P. Echlin. Philadelphia: Westminster, 1970.

Patte, Daniel. *What Is Structural Exegesis?* Philadelphia: Fortress, 1976.

Patterson, Bob E. *Carl F. H. Henry.* Makers of the Modern Theological Mind Series, ed. Bob E. Patterson. Waco, TX: Word, 1983.

Peterson, Gilbert A. "The Christian Teacher" In *Introduction to Biblical Christian Education,* ed. Werner C. Graendorf. Chicago: Moody, 1981.

Piggin, F. S. "Liberal Catholicism." In *EDT.*

Pinnock, Clark H. *Biblical Revelation: The Foundation of Christian Theology.* Chicago: Moody, 1971.

———. *The Scripture Principle.* New York: Harper and Row, 1984.

Polman, A. D. R. *The Word of God According to St. Augustine.* Translated by A. J. Pomernas. Grand Rapids, MI: Eerdmans, 1961.

Ramm, Bernard L. "Hermeneutics." In *BDT.*

———. *Protestant Biblical Interpretation.* 3d rev. ed. Grand Rapids, MI: Baker, 1970.

———. *Witness of the Spirit.* Grand Rapids, MI: Eerdmans, 1959.

Ramsey, Ian T. *Models for Divine Activity.* London: SCM, 1973.

———. *Models and Mystery.* London: Oxford University Press, 1964.

Rayburn, R. S. "Names of Christians." In *EDT.*

Richards, Lawrence O. *Creative Bible Teaching.* Chicago: Moody, 1970.

Richardson, Alan. *The Bible in the Age of Science.* Philadelphia: Westminster, 1961.

Richardson, Peter. "Spirit and Letter: A Foundation for Hermeneutics." *EvQ* 45 (October-December 1973) 208–18.

Robinson, James M. and John B. Cobb, Jr. eds. *New Frontiers in Theology.* Vol. 2, *The New Hermeneutic.* New York: Harper and Row, 1964.

Rogers, Carl R. *Freedom to Learn.* Columbus, OH: Charles E. Merrill, 1969.

Rogers, Jack B. *Scripture in the Westminster Confession: A Problem of Historical Interpretation for American Presbyterianism.* Grand Rapids, MI: Eerdmans, 1967.

Rogers, Jack. B. and Donald K. McKim. *The Authority and Interpretation of the Bible: An Historical Approach.* New York: Harper and Row, 1979.

Runia, Klaas. "The Hermeneutics of the Reformers." *CTJ* 19 (November 1984) 121–52.

Sandeen, Ernest R. "The Princeton Theology." *CH* 31 (September 1962) 307–21.

Saucy, Robert L. *The Bible: Breathed from God.* Victor Know and Believe Series. Wheaton, IL: Victor, 1978.

Schaff, David S. "St. Augustin as an Exegete." In Vol. 6 of *A Select Library of the Nicene and Post-Nicene Fathers of the Christian Church,* ed. Philip Schaff, vii–xii. Grand Rapids, MI: Eerdmans, 1956.

Schaff, Philip. Prolegomena to Saint Chrysostom. Vol. 9 of A Select Library of the Nicene and Post-Nicene Fathers of the Christian Church, ed. Philip Schaff. Grand Rapids, MI: Eerdmans, 1956.

Schaff, David S. "St. Augustin as an Exegete." In Vol. 6 of A Select Library of the Nicene and Post-Nicene Fathers of the Christian Church, ed. Philip Schaff, vii-xii. Grand Rapids, MI: Eerdmans, 1956.

Schleiermacher, Friedrich. *Hermeneutics: The Handwritten Manuscripts.* Translated by James Duke and Jack Forstman Missoula, MT: Scholars Press, 1977.

Schneiders, Sandra M. "Faith, Hermeneutics, and the Literal Sense of Scripture." *TS* 39 (1978) 719–36

Schnucker, R. V. "Neo-Orthodoxy." In *EDT.*

Sergiovanni, Thomas J. and Robert J. Starratt. *Supervision: Human Perspectives.* 4th ed. New York: McGraw-Hill, 1988.

Simpson, E. K. *The Epistles of Paul to the Ephesians and to the Colossians.* NICNT. Grand Rapids, MI: Eerdmans, 1982.

Shelton, Raymond Larry. "Martin Luther's Concept of Biblical Interpretation in Historical Perspective." Th.D. diss., Fuller Theological Seminary, 1974.

Skinner, B. F. *The Technology of Teaching.* New York: Appleton-Century-Crofts, 1968.

Smart, James D. *The Interpretation of Scripture.* Philadelphia: Westminster, 1961.

Soskice, Janet Martin. *Metaphor and Religious Language.* Oxford: Clarendon, 1987.

Stacey, David. *Interpreting the Bible.* New York: Hawthorn Books, 1977.

Stuhlmacher, Peter. "Ex Auditu and the Theological Interpretation of Holy Scripture." *ExAud* 2 (1986) 1–6.

Stuhlmacher, Peter. *Historical Criticism and Theological Interpretation of Scripture: Toward a Hermeneutics of Consent.* Translated by Roy A. Harrisville. Philadelphia: Fortress, 1977.

Thiselton, Anthony C. Personal correspondence with John W. Wyckoff, 30 March 1989. Letter in the hand of John W. Wyckoff. Waxahachie, TX.

———. *The Two Horizons: New Testament Hermeneutics and Philosophical Description.* Grand Rapids, MI: Eerdmans, 1980.

Tompkins, J. P., ed. *Reader-Response Criticism.* Baltimore: John Hopkins University Press, 1980.

Torrance, Thomas F. *God and Rationality.* London: Oxford University Press, 1971.

Turretin, Francis. *The Doctrine of Scripture.* Translated and edited by John W. Beardslee. Grand Rapids, MI: Baker, 1981.

Vidler, Alec R. *The Modernist Movement in the Roman Church: Its Origins and Outcome.* Cambridge: Cambridge University Press, 1934.

Virkler, Henry A. *Hermeneutics: Principles and Processes of Biblical Interpretation.* Grand Rapids, MI: Baker, 1981.

Warfield, B. B. *Calvin and Augustine.* Philadelphia: Presbyterian and Reformed, 1956.

———. "Inspiration." In *The Princeton Theology, 1812-1921: Scripture, Science, and Theological Method from Archibald Alexander to Benjamin Warfield,* ed. and comp. Mark A. Noll. Grand Rapids, MI: Baker, 1983.

Watts, Gary Lynn. "The Theological Method of G. C. Berkouwer." Ph.D. diss., Fuller Theological Seminary, School of Theology, 1981.

Wilhoit, Jim. *Christian Education and the Search for Meaning*. Grand Rapids, MI: Baker, 1986.

Wood, Charles M. "Finding the Life of a Text: Notes on the Explication of Scripture." *SJT* 31 (June 1978) 101–11.

Wood, James D. *The Interpretation of the Bible*. London: Gerald Duckworth, 1958.

Woolfolk, Anita E. *Educational Psychology*. 3rd ed. Englewood Cliffs, NJ: Prentice-Hall, 1987.

Zuck, Roy B. "The Role of the Holy Spirit in Hermeneutics." *BSac* 141 (April-June 1984) 120–30.